Phil Hellmuth's
Texas Hold'em

BOOKS BY PHIL HELLMUTH, JR.

Bad Beats and Lucky Draws
Play Poker Like the Pros

For my parents, Lynn and Phil,
who helped me believe I could do anything and
who supported me even after they freaked out
over my newfound occupation.

To Grandma Aggie,
who loved a good game of cards.

In memory of one of my best friends,
Andy Glazer.

The Universe Conspired to Help

The man had a dream
He knew what he wanted, it seems

Once he was sure in his heart this was it
He vowed someday that he would achieve it

He wasn't quite ready to do his thing
But he felt fairly certain what the
future would bring

When one day the time was right
When he was ready to fight the good fight

He conquered all his excuses and set forth
To take the risk-fraught first step
without any remorse

Once he took the first step down the line
The universe conspired to help make sure
he was fine

He never dreamed he would accomplish so much
That the universe would give him such
incredible luck

Now older and wiser he understood the hardest part
Was convincing himself that it was time to start.

— PHIL HELLMUTH

Contents

INTRODUCTION

The first thing that should be said about this book is this: The content is the same as that in the Texas Hold'em chapters in *Play Poker Like the Pros*, with a few scattered refinements. And there is also an added chapter that should knock your socks off: "How to Win a No-Limit Hold'em Tournament." To me, this new chapter alone should be worth hundreds of dollars, for it will help you to understand the basic game theory that has allowed me to win dozens of no-limit Hold'em tournaments over the years.

I am proud of the fact that hundreds of people have come up to me and said, "Thanks for *Play Poker Like the Pros*. It turned my game around." The Hold'em strategy in that book (and now in this book) is solid and immutable; there is only one mathematically viable way to play winning limit Hold'em. As to pot-limit Hold'em and no-limit Hold'em, many styles work, but you can never travel too far "off campus" (away from the math and fundamentals) without risking crushing failure. This book teaches you the fundamentals, as well as advanced theories, for all forms and levels of Hold'em.

When I penned these chapters, my goal was to help the worldwide public learn, appreciate, and convert to the poker games that the pros play. I felt that it was important to point out that the version of "poker" that most people play on their kitchen tables, with red, white, and blue plastic chips, is a world away from the games that the pros play, in both skill level and complexity. In those home games, people toss their money into virtually every pot, in a sort of "no fold'em" poker that is designed to keep everyone in to the end, and award the luckiest player the pot.

In these types of "poker" games the player who draws the luckiest card on the last possible card dealt wins the pot. Where is the skill in that? Where are the well-timed bluffs, the great calls, the tough lay downs, the judicious reads of opponents, the constantly shifting odds calculations, and the patience involved in the poker games that the pros play? These skills are inherent in real poker games like Seven-Card Stud, Omaha, and the ultimate, Texas Hold'em. Suddenly, people all over the world are playing one-table $5 buy-in (or higher) no-limit Hold'em "tournaments" with their buddies. Nine players lose $5, and when all is said and done, one winner receives the $50 first-place prize. It's the same game in the major tournaments, but there might be 700 buy-ins at $5,000 apiece, a $1 million first-place prize, and 44 others in the money. And it might take four days to get there. No-limit Hold'em, where you can bet any amount at any time—now that's poker!

Although I would like to take some credit for the explosion of poker worldwide, I believe everyone knows that the growth of the game has been fueled by ESPN's World Series of Poker (WSOP), Travel Channel's World Poker Tour (WPT), FOX's new poker coverage, and various internet poker sites such as UltimateBet.com. (By the way, to read about some ballsy bluffs, amazing calls, and memorable "key pots" on the professional poker tour, see my book *Bad Beats and Lucky Draws*.) Of course the WPT deserves most of the credit with its introduction—in this country—of an innovative way of showing the players' hole cards to the TV audience.

Now players worldwide are saying, "I didn't know Hold'em was such an easy game to play. Four rounds of betting, five common cards in the middle of the table, and two hole cards, simple." Simple indeed, unless you actually want to win while playing Hold'em. In this case, there is a learning curve that needs to be mastered. Some of you will learn quickly, scaling the "poker mountain" in short order; others will need more time and effort. In either case, mastering the information in this book is essential to scaling that learning curve. "Texas Hold'em," so the classic characterization goes, "takes five or ten minutes to learn, but a lifetime to master."

Those of you who do master the learning curve for Hold'em, whether quickly or slowly, can expect to see me sooner or later at the WSOP. I'll be the tall one wearing the black UltimateBet.com baseball cap and the Oakley "Phil Hellmuth" brand sunglasses, being cantankerous at times (Poker Brat!) but happily grinding away at a poker hand, at the poker table, while slowly chasing poker history.

One

SKILL VERSUS LUCK IN POKER

Most people today misunderstand poker. Let's be frank: most people know poker from the low-stakes games they now play (or grew up playing) with their family and friends. In these low-stakes home games, luck often plays a much bigger role than skill.

The money to be gained or lost in a home tends to mean next to nothing, and everyone at the table plays almost every hand to the end. The dealer's choice games are often nonstandard, even bizarre variations (often fun) where, for example, deuces, black kings, or one-eyed jacks (or all of them) are wild. In this type of poker game, people just put their money in the middle (in the "pot") and hope to make the best hand. Often, there doesn't seem to be much strategy or thought involved. When the evening winds up, everyone seems to agree that "Johnny sure was hot tonight!" You don't hear anyone saying, "Boy, did Johnny play great tonight. I sure am afraid of him at the poker table."

One reason why luck has such a big role in home-style poker games is that many of the skills we use in pro-style games just don't come into play in a home game. For example, three of the more important skills that we use are being patient in determining which starting hands to play, bluffing, and reading people. Patience, like discipline, is a virtue in many areas of life, and poker is no exception. It is in the nature of professional or tough high-stakes poker games that it is mathematically correct to fold a lot of hands right away. If you are playing too many hands (which equates to too many *bad* hands) in a tough poker game, you will often find yourself "drawing mighty thin," that is, trying to win by catching particular cards that are in short supply.

The plain fact is that if you play too many hands in a pro-level poker game, you just cannot win, certainly not in the long run and probably not even on just one given night, no matter how lucky you are. But if you're playing a lot of hands in a home poker game, you may be in good shape anyway, because the sheer size of the pot will wind up offering you odds sufficient to draw to an inside straight (add a nine, for example, to your 7-8-10-J hand) or another "unlikely to hit" hand. You'll usually lose, but when you do manage to hit the card you need, you're going to win a huge pot.

Further, the number of cards that can complete what you need in the late rounds of a hand in a home game is often larger than one sees in the pro game, because the dealer has designated various wild cards or rules that allow you extra draws or give you chances to buy another card or replace a card.

Because you don't see these big pots and people paying you off with weak hands in a pro poker game, patience is crucial there. In the traditional home-style poker games, patience not only is not as important but may actually clash with the "spirit" of the game—that "We're all here just to have fun and gamble." Playing a more technically informed style may win you more money in a home game, but it might also mean that you're not invited back the next time the game is held! In a casino poker game or an online poker game, of course, you don't need to be concerned that you might not be invited back.

Another key difference between home poker games and the games that the pros play is that bluffing actually succeeds in the pro-style games! In a home game, it's extremely hard to pull off a bluff, because you usually can't bet enough money on the last bet to get your opponents to fold. For 25 cents, someone who is convinced he is beaten is nonetheless willing to throw the two bits into the pot, just to see what you have, and, oops, there goes your attempted bluff. In fact, in most situations in these home games where there is a "bet on the end" (in the last round of action in a given hand), someone is always egging someone else on to be the "sheriff." "Bill, you call that boy and be the sheriff this hand! We can't let him bluff us!"

In the pro game, bluffing is a sound strategy, because in the late stages of a hand there aren't many people who haven't folded. If you've been playing very few hands (that is, patiently), and have seldom been *caught* bluffing during a day of play, then when you do bluff, it's hard for those remaining in the hand to "call you down" through the last bet. Long live the bluff! Bluffing well is an art form, and I will be addressing it at various points throughout this book. The bluff is one of the poker craftsman's tools that is seldom available to players in wild, friendly, low-stakes games.

Another important element in pro poker games is reading your opponents. Are they riding on "hot air" or the real thing? In a lot of home games, there is just so much money in the pot, relative to the size of the final bet, that it makes sense to call that bet. (What do you have to lose?) In pro poker, there is enough money involved, and enough actual thought processes are being utilized, that many situations come up where you can take advantage of a good read—which might arise either from your ability to detect weakness or strength in body language or from your ability to assess the implications of the betting pattern on the hand— and make either a good call or a good fold. But it's hard to read someone who hasn't really been thinking about the hand and can't possibly be nervous about losing $1.75! The skill factor in poker is much higher in the pro game. There is just too much at stake for anyone to rely solely on luck.

Let's take a quick glimpse at the high-stakes poker world, an enterprise that yields several of my friends over a million dollars a year! At this level, too, luck is a factor on any given day, week, or month, but what's different is that if you play better poker than your opponents do, pretty consistently, you'll find that over almost any *two*-month period your winnings have exceeded your losses. Furthermore, if you play better poker than your opponents over a *six*-month period, your results will have moved very solidly in the winning direction. Making a few well-timed bluffs each day will add up to a lot of money each year!

In fact, if an inexperienced poker player were to sit down for a few hours with a group of world-class poker players, he would have virtually no chance to win over even an eight-hour period. This very fact is why five or six top pros might be willing to sit down in the same game with this fellow and each other: the money that even one amateur is likely to contribute makes it worth their while to do battle with so many respected opponents.

This is why so many of the top poker players today drive fine cars and live in palatial homes. Right now, as you're reading this book, there is a $600–$1,200-limit poker game at the Bellagio Casino in Las Vegas and a $400–$800-limit poker game at the Commerce Casino in Los Angeles. There is a $200–$400-limit poker game in Tunica, Mississippi; a $100–$200-limit game at the Taj Mahal in Atlantic City; and a $200–$400-limit game somewhere in New York City. They're playing no-limit poker in San Francisco at the Lucky Chances Casino and high-stakes pot-limit poker in London at the Grosvenor Victoria ("The Vic") and in Paris at the Aviation Club de France. In Vienna, at the Concorde Card Casino, they're playing $75–$150 Seven-Card Stud. (I'll have more to say about these two-figure games in Chapter 2.)

If that's not enough action for you, four nights a week in Los Angeles, there is a $2,000–$4,000-limit Seven-Card Stud game at Larry Flynt's Hustler Club Casino, with Larry himself often playing. In the $400–$800-limit poker game it's easy to take a $25,000 swing in one hour. In the $2,000–$4,000-limit game, where movie stars, former governors, and billionaires play, it's not uncommon for someone to win or lose $250,000 in one night. In these "nosebleed" poker games (the term refers to the altitude of the stakes), strategy, discipline, calculation of the odds, and practiced observation contribute to a game that involves much more skill. Better play wins more hands in the long run.

Imagine yourself facing down Larry Flynt in the $2,000–$4,000 Seven-Card Stud game at the Hustler Club Casino. You're sitting there trying to figure out if he has a strong hand or is full of hot air (bluffing). If you decide right, you will win $25,000, but if you're wrong, it will cost you $25,000. What do you do? You make a good read— of the situation, of the odds, of your opponent— and make an educated guess, rather than a plain old boldfaced guess! The chief difference between your home poker game and the games of the big players is the preponderance of luck in the one and the preponderance of skill in the other. In a game (the Flynt game) where winning just one $4,000 bet a night would mean an income of $16,000 per week (this game runs four days a week), one carefully earned bet can make a great deal of difference.

That's the way things look in the high-stakes "side-game" world at large, but there is even more evidence that skill is present and important in high-stakes poker tournaments today. (When I say "side-game" world, I mean the nontournament poker world.) Why do the same people, by and large, keep winning poker tournaments year after year? They win because they apply finely honed strategies and tactics, calculate and recalculate the odds, read their opponents well, avoid becoming predictable, and know how and when to make a good bluff.

Some of the most famous poker players in the world today have made their names in poker tournaments. Doyle "Texas Dolly" Brunson has nine bracelets (titles) from the World Series of Poker at age 71. I have nine, and so does Johnny "The Oriental Express" Chan. "Amarillo Slim" Preston—whose name is known even to the general public—has seven WSOP titles, depending, as Slim himself would say, on "who does the telling."

I'm proud to say that before the 2004 WSOP I was the all-time leading money winner in World Series history, with over $3.5 million won. In fact, at that time no one else had crossed the $3 million mark other than Johnny Chan and me. (He beat me there! But I'll win the race to $7 million!) Although the same people don't win *all* the poker tournaments, by the time year's end rolls around, the same people always seem to end up having won several tournaments, year in and year out. This is one of the appealing aspects of poker tournaments: the record is out there for everyone to see; some players are consistently successful, and others are not. (The side games, though very lucrative, keep no records.)

If serious poker were a game where luck predominates, this would not and could not happen. Everyone involved would win about the same number of tournaments as everyone else (as tends to happen in slot tournaments or craps tournaments), and no one would make (or lose) any serious money. But that's not what years and years of proven, recorded results show.

Two

TEXAS HOLD'EM: SETUP AND BASIC PLAY

This chapter will introduce you to Texas Hold'em, commonly referred to as "Hold'em," the most popular poker game in the world today. The chapter should teach you enough to allow you to sit down and play the game without needing to ask your fellow players a lot of what feel like embarrassing questions. (Beginners, by the way, shouldn't feel embarrassed about asking questions; everyone has to start somewhere.) Later chapters will guide you through the subtleties of beginning, intermediate, and advanced strategy.

Learning the basic structure, or format, of Texas Hold'em is easy. This doesn't mean, though, that there isn't a great deal of strategy involved: there is. But the way the game is constructed is fairly simple, compared with a game like chess, where you must learn how to move many different pieces, or even compared with many wild home poker games, where the rules for a game often take way too long to explain. ("Seven-Card Stud, threes and nines are wild, but if you catch a three face up you must match the size of the pot to keep the card or else fold. You can buy an extra card on the end for $20 or replace a card on the end for $10, and if you catch a four face up you get an extra card free.")

If you were to walk into a card room or a friend's house to play Hold'em, and hadn't seen Hold'em before, you would want some explanation. But once you understand the pattern of the deal, whose turn it is to bet, how much that player can bet, and what all of the options are (*checking*, *calling*, *betting*, *raising*, and *folding*) during the play of a hand, then you'll have a solid foundation for understanding the basic strategy tips you'll find in the later chapters. After reading (and absorbing) this chapter, you'll be able to introduce Hold'em into your own Saturday night poker game, although I wouldn't recommend playing it for much money until you've learned some strategy!

THE ROLE OF THE DEALER

In most poker games, including Texas Hold'em,

the deal rotates clockwise. When you're playing at home, you simply change dealers after each hand, moving the deal around the table clockwise, one player to the next, but in a casino there is a professional dealer at the table who deals every hand. The dealer, whether at home or in the casino, will shuffle, deal, keep the bets right, manage the pot, and help control the tempo of the game. A good dealer will keep things moving, both by dealing quickly and reliably and by diplomatically encouraging action from the slower players. (In the home game, of course, the dealer is also a player.)

THE ROLE OF THE BUTTON: WHOSE DEAL IS IT?

In "casino-style" Hold'em, the dealer uses a white plastic puck roughly 2 inches in diameter, called the *button*, to indicate who the dealer would be if the game were being played without a professional dealer. Usually, the puck has the word "dealer" printed on each side. Instead of simply passing the deck one player to the left after each hand, as you do in home poker games, you sit still while the professional dealer moves the button one spot to the left after each hand, and then deals. Why bother with this step? For one thing, no one has to wonder, or ask, whose deal it is. More important, the "dealer" (the player sitting behind the button) acts last in Hold'em in each round of betting and thus has a significant positional advantage, because (among other things) that player has more information available to him when it's his turn to bet than the players who had to act first. The use of the button ensures that each player—though never actually dealing the cards—gets a chance to enjoy that advantageous position once in each round of hands. (And of course with eight or more players at the table, next-to-last is a pretty good spot to be in too.)

The button also enables us to determine the order of play for each hand. The player seated to the left of the button acts first (except on the very first betting round), and the player who owns the button acts last (with that same first-round exception). We turn to those exceptions next. By the way, I recommend that you use a button even when you're playing Hold'em in your home poker game, and dealers are truly dealing. It helps remind people who dealt, and whose turn it is to deal next, and I think it also makes for an easier transition to playing casino Hold'em.

THE TWO "BLINDS"
TO THE LEFT OF THE BUTTON

Before the first round of betting, and before any cards are dealt, those first two players, directly to the left of the button, post (place in front of them) what we call the *blinds*. We call these the "blind" bets because those two players must invest them in the pot, in preset amounts, before they can look at any cards. Immediately after the button, we have the *small blind*, which is usually, but not always, set at half the size of the next blind, which is called the *big blind*.

The size of the blinds is determined by the size of the game. The small blind is usually half a small bet, and the big blind is usually a full small bet. In a hypothetical $2–$4 game, the small blind would be $1 and the big blind $2. Limit Hold'em games (we'll get to no-limit Hold'em a bit later) are thus defined by their bet sizes. For example, you might play $2–$4 Hold'em, or $10–$20 Hold'em, or whatever. In the $2–$4 game, all bets and raises during the first two betting rounds are made in $2 increments, and all bets and raises during the final two betting rounds (the third and fourth rounds) are made in $4 increments (you can't bet, say, 50 cents, or $3, on any round). As you might expect, in the $10–$20 game all bets and raises during the first two betting rounds are made in $10 increments, and all bets and raises during the final two betting rounds are made in $20 increments. In Las Vegas, the maximum number of bets is five, unless there are just two players left in the pot— those two players can then raise and reraise each other until the money in front of one of them is gone.

TWO CARDS ARE DEALT TO EACH PLAYER, FACEDOWN

Once the blinds are posted in the pot (directly in front of the players posting them), the dealer deals two cards facedown to each player, one card at a time. The position of the button and the two blinds determines whose turn it is to act first. (The illustration shows a poker table with players sitting around it, the blinds posted, and two down cards in front of each player.) The cards that have been dealt to you are your own "private" cards, often called *hole cards*; take care not to let your neighbors see them. They belong to you and you only for the duration of one hand, and as soon as you see them, you should begin assessing the strength

"Pocket rockets" (aces) for the reader!

of your hand. Later on in the hand, the dealer will be dealing cards faceup in the middle of the table, where everyone can see them. This isn't a mistake: these later cards are *community cards*, and I'll explain how they fit into the dealing and the betting in just a moment.

THE PLAYER TO THE LEFT OF THE TWO BLINDS ACTS FIRST

Now the blinds have been posted, and the dealer has dealt out each player's first two cards. Then, to begin the first round of play, the player to the left of the big blind acts first. Technically, the two blind bettors have "acted" first, by posting their bets, but because their "action" is involuntary, the player sitting to the left of the big blind is really the first player who faces a decision, and the first who will take some kind of voluntary action, as he sees fit.

Note that the blinds are posted only before the very first betting round. In the following rounds of that hand, the remaining player closest to the button's left is the first to act.

During the first betting round, the player to the left of the posted blinds has just three options: calling the bet (matching the big blind), raising the bet (to exactly double the big blind), or folding his hand. (All calls or raises are part of the pot, but are placed in front of the players making them, so that other players can keep track of who has put in what: when the betting on a round is done, then the dealer drags them all into the pot.) Usually, players fold by gently tossing or sliding their cards into the middle of the table facedown, without comment; but a verbal declaration—saying simply, "I fold"—is also acceptable and is considered binding: you must then release your hand. Although poker involves a great deal of deception, if you state that you're taking an action, you must follow through. You can't say "I fold" and then, after hearing a sigh of relief, push chips into the pot to make a bet. Similarly, you can't say "I raise" and then toss in your cards instead.

The next player to act on this first round has the same three options as the preceding player: he may call, raise, or fold. The following player to act also has the same options—call, raise, or fold—and so on until the action in the first round of betting is complete. Once the action is completed, the first round is over and the dealer drags the bets into the pot. (By the way, if you follow my advice in the chapters on strategy, you will be folding frequently on the first round of betting, as Hold'em is a real game of patience.)

ONE MORE CIRCUMSTANCE OF THE FIRST ROUND OF PLAY

The only other betting rule you need to know about in the first round is that the two players in the blinds have the option of raising the bet, just as anyone else in the hand does when it is his turn to act. In an unraised pot in our hypothetical $2–$4 game, the small blind may come into play by adding $1 to complete his bet to the full $2 size, or $3 ($3 + $1 = $4) to complete one full raise, and the big blind, even though he already has his $2 in, has the option of raising the pot another $2. In fact, a pro dealer will always ask the big blind if he wishes to raise it if the big blind hasn't made a motion one way or the other. I know that this may sound complicated at first, but after you've played about four hands it will seem very simple. (My parents played in a poker tournament the day after I taught them how to play, in September 2000.) Put more simply, when it's your turn to act during a Hold'em hand, you will always have the option of betting (when no one else has bet yet), checking (when no one has bet and you don't want to bet either), calling, raising, or folding.

THE SECOND ROUND OF BETTING

After the first round of play is complete, the dealer flips three community cards faceup in the middle of the table. These are available for use by everyone (as we shall see), and they stay there throughout the hand. We call the three community cards (and the moment they are dealt) the *flop*. In every hand of Hold'em, the flop is a signal moment; for each player still in the hand, these three new community cards are likely to confirm his high hopes for the hand or all but shatter them, since there are

Hold 'em Flop
You, the reader, have flopped three aces!

just two other cards still to come. Since the blinds are used only during the first round of betting, the first remaining player who is closest to the left of the button begins the action in the second round. You might suppose that this is the same player who had to post the small blind before any cards were dealt, but it's quite possible, even likely, that the small blind, the big blind, and other players have folded during the first round, either because these early-position players didn't like their own hands or because someone else raised.

This person, the one who begins the second-round action and has seen the flop, may now check (make no bet at all, but not fold his hand either; in effect, he is saying, "I'm not betting right now, but I retain my option to call bets or even to raise, later in the hand"), fold (you should never fold until someone has made a bet that you would otherwise have to at least call), or bet. It's possible that everyone will check, the pot remaining just as it was; in this case, too, this round of play is complete. But the appearance of the three flop cards on the table will change everyone's view of the hand.

THE THIRD ROUND OF BETTING

After the second round of play is complete, the dealer flips up a fourth community card faceup.

Hold 'em 4th Street

This card, which also stays on the table throughout the hand, is usually called either *the turn* or *fourth street*. Then the third round of betting begins. Again, the person closest to the left of the button who still has a live hand (hasn't folded) begins the betting, and, take note, *the stakes are now doubled*. (The bets are larger, but there are, in nearly all hands, fewer players—the others have folded.)

THE FOURTH ROUND OF BETTING

After the third round of betting is complete, the dealer flips up the fifth and last community card, faceup in the middle of the table. This card is usually called either *fifth street* or (much more often) *the river*. Now we have the five community cards in the middle of the table plus the two that you have in your hand: seven cards total. Each of you will settle on the best five cards out of the seven available to you (including one, two, or neither of the cards in your hand) to make your best possible poker hand (see Appendix). Now the fourth and final round of betting begins. After this round is completed, you will all flip up your *hole cards* to determine who has the best hand. Usually, once someone has shown a hand that no one else can beat, no one else bothers showing his hand at this point. (Sometimes a player who feels he got unlucky on the turn or the river may show a good hand that "went bad." We call this a "sympathy show.")

A SHORT REVIEW OF WHAT A HAND OF LIMIT TEXAS HOLD'EM LOOKS LIKE

There are four rounds of betting in limit Hold'em. The first round plays out before the flop (before the first three community cards are dealt, faceup), and on that first round you can bet and raise in one-unit increments. The second round occurs after the flop, and you can still bet and raise in exactly one-unit increments. The third round of betting occurs after the fourth card (fourth street or the turn) is flipped up, and now all bets and raises are made in two-unit increments. The fourth and final round of betting occurs after the fifth and final community card (the river) has been flipped up, and again you can bet and raise in two-unit increments.

Starting with the setup that I've illustrated (on page 24) in an eight-handed limit Hold'em hand, let's run through a $2–$4 sample hand. The dealer has dealt out two cards each, facedown, and the small blind of $1 and the big blind of $2 have been posted. Player one (P1) folds his hand, P2 (who holds, let's say, ace-jack, a hand that we will be referring to as A-J) raises, making it $4 to call the bet. P3, P4, and P5 all fold. P6, holding K-Q (king-queen), calls $4. The dealer and the small blind (SB) fold. The big blind (BB) calls the bet holding 9-8: because he already has $2 invested in the pot, it costs him only $2 more to see the flop. Now the dealer turns up a flop of 2-4-9.

Although P2 held the best preflop hand with his A-J, fortunes have changed on the flop. The player who sat in the BB with 9-8 is now the only player who has a pair (though he has no way to be certain of this), and suspecting that his pair might be the best hand, he bets $2. P2 and P6 somewhat loosely and stubbornly call the $2 bet, even though neither yet has a pair.

The turn card proves to be a ten, for a *board* of 2-4-9-10, and although the BB is a bit concerned by both this *overcard* (a board card higher than his pair) and the fact that two players called his opening bet, he decides to stay aggressive and bets $4 (recall that third-round bets are doubled). P2 folds (wisely, because there are now only six cards in the deck that can save him—three aces and three jacks), and P6 (who now needs a jack for a straight, or a queen or a king to make him a pair)

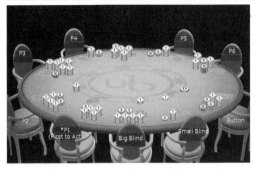

First round of betting—P2 raises

calls the $4 bet. P6's call is good, because with any jack, queen, or king probably winning for him, he has ten probable winning cards (which are usually called *outs* in poker slang).

Fate isn't always just, however, and even though the odds were against it, the river card is a Q, for a 2-4-9-10-Q board, and the BB simply checks, figuring there is a good chance that if he wasn't already beaten by a starting hand like J-J or A-10, he is now vulnerable to any hand containing a queen. Now P6 bets $4, and BB sighs and calls the $4 bet. P6 shows his Q-K, for a pair of queens, and BB shows a 9-8 for his pair of nines. The pot is awarded to P6, who, perversely enough, had the second-best hand before the flop and the worst hand on both the flop and the turn!

TWO IMPORTANT ASPECTS OF HOLD'EM ETIQUETTE

The game does involve some points of etiquette, and I would be remiss not to mention two issues at this point. For one, be sure you avoid "slow-rolling" an opponent in a casino. When you're virtually certain you hold the winning hand (and it won't take you very long in your poker education before you know when you probably hold the winner!), and you then hesitate for a moment before you flip your hand up—clearly grandstanding and probably trying to make your opponent think he holds the winning hand—that's slow-rolling.

Usually, a hesitation on the end by the bettor means that the bettor's hand is weak, and the players hate it when you then flip your strong hand up slowly. When a player perceives that he has won the pot, because you've stalled, but then, "bang," you tear his heart out and take the pot away from him, you're not making a friend; indeed, you're probably making an enemy who will have an elephant's memory and will look for revenge someday.

Another important point of etiquette is to be sure you always act in turn. Players are supposed to act one at a time, in a clockwise direction. If you look at your hand and realize you have nothing and are planning to fold, you still have a duty to the other players to sit there and look as interested or uninterested as you usually do, rather than folding out of turn. Why? I could give you many examples, but they mainly add up to this: your premature fold would give the other players information to which they aren't entitled. Your early display of weakness may encourage someone to play who might otherwise have been bluffed out by the play of an opponent.

This may seem a bit picky, but I promise you that the further you progress in your poker career, the more important you will realize this is, and the more likely it will be that at some time in your career someone will cost *you* a pot by giving away *his* weakness too soon. Suppose, for example, that you've correctly figured out that one of your opponents has nothing. You then decide to bluff at the pot with your own very weak hand in order to get rid of a third opponent whose turn to act arrives before the opponent that you think is weak can act. The man you are bluffing starts to study you and begins to fold, partly out of fear of your bet, and partly fearing that even if you're bluffing, the opponent behind him may have him beat. Now if that later opponent—the one you read as being weak—folds out of turn, and the opponent that you so skillfully bluffed at decides to call you, instead of folding, you have just lost a pot that you would have won, if only your weak opponent had played in turn!

INTRODUCING LIMIT HOLD'EM INTO YOUR PRIVATE GAME

If you've followed me to this point, you'll be able to play Hold'em in your own home game. At first it might seem hard, but after less than an hour of playing Hold'em, you'll have the basics down.

How much should you play for? In $1–$2-limit Hold'em, the big winner for the night might win $100. (Notice that this figure is 50 times the largest bet allowed in the game; expressing expectations in terms of *x* number of big bets per session or per hour is pretty common in poker.) But $20 to $40 wins (just 10 to 20 big bets) will be far more common. Wins equivalent to more than 50 big bets do happen, but they are very rare, and you could play a long time without seeing one, and a much longer time without experiencing one yourself! If you've understood what I've been saying about predicting wins and losses in terms of number of big bets won, you can probably figure out that in a $2–$4 game you can expect the big winner to win around $200, but that more commonly you will see a lot of $40 to $80 wins and losses at this limit (again, 10 to 20 big bets).

So what limit should your poker game have? You'll have to answer this for yourself. You can play with a limit of 25 cents and 50 cents if you're a poor college student and take $5–$10 swings on average. If you're an investment banker, perhaps you would enjoy playing with a limit of $300–$600, with average swings hitting $6,000 to $12,000 and the big winner sometimes winning $60,000! If your group normally takes swings of about $20, then I would suggest that you play at that level (75 cents and $1.50) for Hold'em. Remember that the stakes can be changed very easily just by changing the size of the blinds. Note that if your group really plays Hold'em poorly, then the swings will be about twice as high. Speaking of playing Hold'em poorly brings me to the next section.

THE ADVANTAGE OF POSITION

As I've been teaching you the setup and basic play for Hold'em, I have referred to the advantage of position many times. Having position in Hold'em, thus being one of the last players to act in a hand, is a great advantage. You can just sit back and wait for everyone else in front of you to act. If an opponent bets and you are strong, then you can raise, effectively doubling the amount of money that is put into the pot and raising other strong hands out of the pot by making it twice as expensive for them to call. If your opponent bets and you are weak, then you can fold. If your opponent checks (in this case he is showing you some weakness), now you can act on your hand accordingly. By acting last, you get a better feel for the strength of your opponents' hands. I will really get into the differences between being in or out of position in the chapters on strategy.

NO-LIMIT TEXAS HOLD'EM STRUCTURE: THE CADILLAC!

No-limit Hold'em (NLH) is considered the Cadillac of poker games, because most professionals believe it involves more skill than any other modern-day poker game. The structure of no-limit Hold'em is exactly like that of limit Hold'em, except that when it is your turn to act you can bet any amount at any time during any hand! In plainer language, the game is still dealt the same way, but now you can bet any amount at any time. It's pretty exciting to watch someone push a mountain of chips into one pot! At the World Championships of 2001, I pushed in almost $1 million in one hand, and lost!

After a flop of Q-9-3, I bet out $70,000 and Carlos Mortenson raised it to $270,000 to go. I studied awhile and then reraised all of my chips (about $1 million total) with Q-10 (top pair), thinking that Carlos had at best Q-J, and that he couldn't call me even if he did have Q-J. Carlos did have Q-J, and he made an incredible call on me! No-limit Hold'em is treacherous; I had survived for five days in the World Championships, only to get blown out in a single spectacular hand!

POT-LIMIT HOLD'EM

The structure of pot-limit Hold'em (PLH) is the same, except that the betting is limited to the size of the pot. So if the blinds are $10–$20, and you want to *raise the pot* (make the maximum raise), you can call $20 and then raise $50 more ($10 small blind + $20 big blind + your $20 call = $50), making it $70 to go. When it is your turn to act, you can always bet or raise the size of the pot. Because it is almost always correct to bet the size of the pot, you see a lot of big bets in pot-limit Hold'em—especially on the last round of betting when the pot is huge—just as in no-limit Hold'em.

Because the differences between PLH and NLH aren't very significant, especially to beginning and intermediate players, I'll treat the games the same way in the chapters on strategy. However, I will point out some of the subtle differences in strategy along the way.

Phil Hellmuth's Texas Hold'em

Phil Hellmuth, Jr.

○ Collins

An Imprint of HarperCollins*Publishers*

HarperCollins books may be purchased for educational, business, or sales promotional use. For information, please write: Special Markets Department, HarperCollins Publishers, 10 East 53rd Street, New York, NY 10022.

FIRST EDITION

ISBN-10: 0-06-083460-9
ISBN-13: 978-0-06-083460-9

05 06 07 08 09 ❖/ WOR 10 9 8 7 6 5 4 3 2 1

Three

LIMIT HOLD'EM: BEGINNERS' STRATEGY

I remember well my introduction to Texas Hold'em at the Memorial Union on the campus of the University of Wisconsin (UW). I was a poor (OK, broke!) undergraduate student at UW then, with nothing to lose (literally). Amazingly enough, the game was played right in the middle of the Student Union, infamous for its relaxed mores. For some reason, the powers that be didn't think students should be playing poker there, but because we used some old Austrian coins as chips, instead of the usual red, white, and blue plastic chips that were the standard for the time, none of the authorities seemed to notice what we were playing. The game of choice offered additional camouflage: we were playing Texas Hold'em instead of the much more easily recognized Seven-Card Stud.

I fancied myself a great poker player at the time, and when I heard about the game, I hurried down to play. Of course, I wasn't even a good player then, because I'd had very little experience. It seems that everyone overrates himself when it comes to playing poker!

The players were quite an eclectic mix: taxi drivers, students, professors, lawyers, and even a prominent psychiatrist. When I sat down and bought in for $20, I was warmly welcomed by the group, because every game needs some new blood (and fresh cash) once in a while. I quickly learned that I had a lot to learn about Texas Hold'em. I had a great time, but my $20 didn't last long, and it was all I could afford to risk. Although I didn't know much about poker yet, I at least had the good sense not to risk more than I could afford to lose, or borrow money I'd have trouble paying back.

Still, I thought I was gaining a feel for the game and its nuances, and, with so much money flying around down there, I thought I might one day begin paying my tuition with my poker profits. So I struck up an acquaintance with the best player in the game and set out to learn how to play Texas Hold'em the right way.

My new acquaintance, Tuli Haromy, ended up becoming my best friend for the next eight years.

He was also the best player and banker for the game. (The banker is responsible for passing out chips, cashing checks, judging how much he can lend various players, and making sure that everyone is paid at the end of the night.) That made sense, because the best player has a vested interest in making sure the other players have access to cash to play with (and lose to him). It turned out that Tuli was originally from Las Vegas, which explains why we were playing Hold'em in Madison, Wisconsin, in the first place. Without someone with Tuli's Las Vegas background, the chances of finding a Hold'em game in Madison in the early 1980s would have been slim to none!

Tuli had a basic theory about Hold'em: "Tight is right." "Tight" means that you drop out of most hands before the flop. It was good advice. After studying the game with Tuli's tutoring and playing with the group for about three months, I found that I'd surpassed Tuli and become the best player in the game. After all, I had no job and no money, which meant that I had a lot of time on my hands and a strong motivation to learn the game. The amount of money I was winning each week was pretty good, too. In fact, from my modest perspective, the money was phenomenal. After about 18 months, I'd put more than $20,000 in the bank, and I paid off all my student loans! A bigger poker game on campus included mostly successful faculty and staff members, doctors, and lawyers. The money, combined with the fact that my ego felt great competing with and beating successful PhDs, JDs, and doctors twenty years older than I was, caused me to devote a lot more time and energy to learning Texas Hold'em.

While I was crushing the games in Madison, I began developing my own basic theory of Texas Hold'em. I had taken Tuli's theory and moved on: supertight was better than tight. In other words, playing even fewer hands than Tuli had suggested was the way to go. Another skill I had developed was an ability to read my opponents (to analyze how strong or weak their hands were, from subtle clues of behavior). Reading players, though, is a more advanced concept, so for now let's just take a look at my theory: "Supertight is right."

To make "supertight" something that you can sink your teeth into, I'll begin by identifying my top ten hands for Hold'em—the ten strongest Hold'em hands out there. I'll then teach you how to play those top ten hands before the flop, on the flop, on fourth street, and, finally, on the river—in other words, on all four rounds of betting. I'll teach you how to use well-timed raises on the flop to gain information that will help you judge, in the final rounds, whether or not your opponents have you beat. I'll show you how to make good use of that information when you're on fourth street. Finally, I'll show you that folding your hand on the river is usually not a good idea, because of the amount of money that's already in the pot by then.

Before we get into analyzing tactics in actual hands, I'll also introduce certain "animal types" that describe many of the people you will be playing against. Through examples, I'll show you when to raise, reraise, call, or fold your hand, depending on what types of "animals" your opponents seem to be, and thus what their tendencies are likely to be.

If you can truly absorb all the information I'll be offering in this chapter, and act on it under game conditions, you will already be capable of beating most small-limit Texas Hold'em players all over the world! I will now teach you how to play limit Texas Hold'em—the variation of Texas Hold'em in which the size of the bet in each round is preset. This is the most popular poker game in the world today.

Be sure you have read Chapter 2 before you read this chapter. In this chapter you will learn:

➤ Preflop limit Hold'em for beginners: the top
ten hands only.
➤ My "animal types": jackal, mouse, elephant,
lion, and eagle.
➤ How to play the flop for beginners: the power
of the raise.
➤ How to play A-K on the flop.
➤ How to play the top ten hands on fourth street.
➤ How to play the river: call because of pot odds.

PREFLOP LIMIT HOLD'EM: LESSONS FOR BEGINNERS, TOP TEN HANDS ONLY

To begin with, I recommend playing only the top
ten hands and folding on all others. The top ten
are, in order of relative promise: A-A, K-K, Q-Q,
A-K, J-J, 10-10, 9-9, 8-8, A-Q, and finally 7-7.
Experience has shown me that these are the
strongest starting hands in limit Hold'em. This
beginning "strategy for survival" is designed to keep
you in the game while you learn the more subtle
techniques that are necessary to beat tougher
games, or to extract more money from weak
games. And in *some* games using just this strategy
will make you a winner. With this patient strategy

♣♥ "Top Ten" Hands in Hold'em ♦♠

1. A-A
2. K-K
3. Q-Q
4. A-K
5. J-J
6. 10-10
7. 9-9
8. 8-8
9. A-Q
10. 7-7

Phil's top ten hands in Hold 'em

alone, and really not much else in the way of poker instruction, I was able to crush the games in Madison. What happens is that when you consistently play only the top ten hands, your opponents will begin to fear your bets and raises because they'll see that you're always playing something powerful. This fear gives you some leeway to make a few different plays later on, when you've absorbed the intermediate and more advanced advice I'll be giving you later. In other words, the "top ten hands" strategy teaches the right fundamentals. You will need these fundamentals when you do add some intermediate and advanced strategy to your arsenal, because playing supertight alone just won't get the pots in these tougher games: the good hands don't come along often enough, and perhaps even more important, you risk becoming a bit too predictable.

When you break limit Hold'em down to its basic elements, good game theory suggests that you wait for big starting hands before you get involved in a hand, because the blinds are relatively small compared with the size of the pots, unless you're playing in a very tight game (which is rare at low stakes). It may seem a bit boring to play only these top ten hands; after all, most of you play poker just to have a good time and socialize—that is, for entertainment. Fair enough, but if you want to win the money, then you need to show some patience and entertain yourself in another way. And, anyway, how entertaining is it to play all the hands and lose most of them?

In general, I recommend playing the top ten hands regardless of your position in the betting order or the number of bets it will cost you to get involved in the hand. Always raise with these hands, no matter what it costs you to get involved. Of course, if you have a lot of evidence to suggest that your 7-7 is beaten (perhaps the tightest player in the game has just re-re-reraised the hand, making it, as we say, "four bets to go"), then you might do well to fold the hand. But in general, playing these hands aggressively is a good way to play Hold'em.

I know that you're probably thinking right now, "Is it really that easy? All I have to do is play Phil's top ten hands?" The answer is basically yes, at least as far as your *starting requirements* (your first two cards) are concerned! Yes, because it will be easy for you to play before the flop (on the first round of betting) when all you have to remember is to play only the top ten. (Playing after the flop is much more complicated, I'm afraid; but don't worry, we'll cover that as well.)

In what follows I'll be giving you a number of examples of hands that will help you understand the best courses of action for a beginning player to take. But before I give you these examples, it's time to introduce those "animals" I promised you. I cannot go much further in teaching you how to play poker without characterizing some of the personality types that you will inevitably face as you play Texas Hold'em, because no matter how much you may want to think of Hold'em as a card game played by people, in many respects it is even more valid to think of it as a game about people that happens to be played with cards. This becomes more and more true as the stakes get higher and the games get tougher.

PHIL'S "ANIMAL TYPES"

These are the five animals: the *mouse*, *lion*, *jackal*, *elephant*, and *eagle*. I have created these animals because they seem to be the most common types out there right now.

The mouse is like your old aunt Edna, a conservative type who probably wouldn't even approve of your reading this book. The mouse— like you—plays only the top ten hands but hates to invest any money with a hand as weak as 7-7 or 8-8. The mouse hardly ever raises someone else's bet; but when he does raise, look out, because he has the goods!

The lion is a tough competitor who plays fairly tight poker but doesn't limit himself to the top ten hands. He bluffs with excellent timing and seems to know when the other players are trying to bluff him. Though he plays pretty tight, he's occasionally out on a limb with a bluff or a semibluff. You could do worse than play like the lion.

The jackal is loose and wild, and some days it seems as though he's just giving his money away. Because he's involved in so many pots and raises so

Phil's animal types

often, his play can take some pretty big swings. The jackal's logic seems at odds with the logic of all the other players. He just seems crazy! (He's what many of us in poker call a megalomaniac, or sometimes just maniac.) The jackal can hurt you and himself too with his crazy play, because he puts in so many bets. But there is some method to his madness. He's good at raising the pots at the right times (his style of play gives him many occasions to think about what's going on), and when he does at last win a pot, it's generally huge! If a jackal runs hot by catching good cards for a while, you may become convinced that he's the best player in the world, but when his cards come back to earth, he can lose money as fast as he won it.

The elephant is fairly loose (which means he plays a lot of pots) and seems to be from Missouri, the "Show me" state. He's what we refer to in poker as a "calling station": he never folds when he is supposed to fold, because he doesn't ever believe that you have the goods. Because he's impossible to bluff, no one with much experience ever tries to bluff him—with one exception: can you guess who that is? The elephant keeps feeding the other players his chips, slowly but surely. The elephant isn't very sharp and isn't a very dangerous opponent for most players, but he seems to do well against the jackal, because the jackal keeps on trying to bluff the elephant.

Finally, we have the eagle. The eagle is a rare bird, and you might not ever play with him, because he's one of the top 100 poker players in the world. You'll find the eagle wherever high-stakes poker is played. He flies around high in the sky and swoops down to eat other animals' chips when he's hungry! You'll find the eagles competing every year at the World Series of Poker

(WSOP), trying to win world championships and the money and prestige that come with winning them—if not in the tournaments, then perhaps in the big-money side games the WSOP always generates. Learning how to play like an eagle is a lofty and worthwhile goal, but it is beyond the scope of this book. (In fact, if you're able to absorb everything in this book, then perhaps I'll see you sitting across the table from me soon.)

Now that we've pondered the personalities of most of the animals (players) that you'll be playing against, it's time to move forward with some examples of how to play the top ten hands to perfection. (As we proceed, you'll see the value of recognizing these personality types.) Again, the basic premise in playing the top ten hands is this: always raise or reraise with these hands before the flop, no matter what the action has been before it's your turn to act. (While I lay out these examples, I'll begin to weave into the equations some ways to play the hands somewhat differently, depending on which animals you're playing against.)

RAISING WITH A TOP TEN HAND IN LATE POSITION

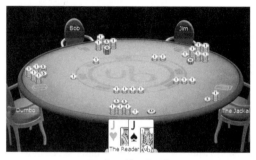

Reraise—"four bets"

The game is $2–$4 at your local bar. You hold J-J on the button. The player in the first position (see illustration) has raised, making it two bets, or $4, to go, and the jackal, in the second position, has reraised (The jackal reraised! What a surprise!), making it three bets, or $6, to go. You then raise it again to make it four bets, or $8, to go. This hand is easy enough to play because you have one of those top ten hands and also have the advantage of late position.

BEWARE OF THE MOUSE

The game is $5–$10 at the local businessmen's club. You have 9-9 in the small blind, and the jackal, in the third position, has raised it to two bets, or $10, to go. Then the lion, in the fourth position, makes it three bets, or $15, to go. Now, the mouse on the button makes it four bets to go! Yikes, what to do? You know that the lion probably has a strong hand, but the mouse making it four bets, even over the top of the lion? That is big trouble!

You decide that the mouse probably has A-A or K-K, and you throw your hand away right then and there, because you figure that you're a $4\frac{1}{2}$-to-1 underdog (a small pair is roughly a $4\frac{1}{2}$-to-1 underdog against a big pair). I know that I've said you should always play these hands, but sometimes a little discretion is the better part of valor. If no animal personalities had entered the picture, you could play this hand—but poker is about people as well as game theory. Deciding to call the four bets in this case wouldn't actually be foolhardy—but it would be a pretty weak play, one that would lose money over the long run. Many players who consider themselves experts would call this a terrible play, but they're forgetting to consider the very large pots you're likely to win in such cases if you do happen to "flop a set" (three of a kind, in this case three nines).

RERAISING THE JACKAL WITH A TOP TEN HAND IN CYBERSPACE

The game is $10-$20 limit (which means you could win or lose $1,000 on any given night) at UltimateBet.com, an online poker site. You have A-K in the second position and with your raise you make it $20 to go. The elephant, in the fourth position, calls the $20 (that's what elephants do, after all), and then the jackal makes it $30 to go from the small blind. What should you do? You make it $40 to go, figuring that you have both the jackal and the elephant beat. The elephant has probably called with a hand too weak to call with, and the jackal has probably raised with a hand too weak to raise with.

If either of them has a pair, then you will need to make a hand, but this is still a good time to play aggressively. Making it four bets here is an especially good play, because the jackal could have anything. And putting in those extra bets now will make the pot so large that you'll probably be forced to play the hand farther than you might want to, making it easier to call the jackal down with ace high. This is good, because no one will be able to bluff you off your A-K if you miss the flop. The pot will be large enough to make it right to call even if you miss the flop.

A TOP TEN HAND AGAINST A MOUSE

The game is $15–$30 limit at the Mirage poker room in Las Vegas. The jackal in seat one raises the bet, making it $30 to go. The mouse on the button makes it three bets, or $45 to go. You have K-K in the big blind, so you make it $60 to go. Yes, the mouse's raise is ominous, but you have K-K, the second-best-possible hand, and you need to raise with it no matter what the hand looks like otherwise.

POCKET ACES

You have A-A in any position before the flop. Put in as many bets as you can before the flop, regardless of what your opponents do! This is the best possible hand in Hold'em!

KINGS, QUEENS, AND A-K

You have K-K, Q-Q, or A-K in any position before the flop. Again, put as many bets out there as you can before the flop! With any of these you have one of the four best hands in Hold'em!

POCKET JACKS

You have J-J before the flop, in any position. OK, you have the fifth-best hand in Hold'em, and in general I would say never fold this hand before the flop in limit Hold'em. But there may come a time or two, as you become a lion, when you choose to fold this hand before the flop. Maybe, for example, the tightest mouse on the planet has made it four bets to go, and you just have a strong feeling that you're beat. After all, what hand would encourage the tightest player in the world to make it four bets to go? Probably A-A or K-K. But because this is the beginners' section, I'd advise you to put in your four bets anyway; when you are a lion you will know when the time is right to fold this hand.

Before the flop, then, successful play in Hold'em is pretty darn easy using the top-ten-hands strategy. In general, you raise or reraise every time you have a top ten hand, and you fold the rest of your hands. The exceptions are: when a mouse makes a raise or reraise (two bets or three bets), a lion makes it three bets (a reraise), or an elephant makes it three bets (since it is out of the ordinary for the elephant ever to bet his own hand). In these cases, you might want to back off if your top ten hand is 9-9, 8-8, 7-7, or A-Q.

Notice that I'm not diagramming the way you should play every hand. There are just too many variables for me to attempt that. The fact is that the play of some of these hands depends on the opponents involved. But I've given you a few things to think about, and you will develop many more things to think about as you gain more experience and a greater feel for the game. It's time now to move on toward the next step in playing a limit Texas Hold'em hand: how a beginner should play limit Hold'em on the flop.

PLAYING THE FLOP FOR HOLD'EM BEGINNERS: THE POWER OF THE RAISE

The principle that I am going to teach you in this section is how to use a raise on the flop to find out "where you are at" in a hand. I'll show you how to use the raise or reraise on the flop to gain information, so as to learn, perhaps, whether you have the best hand or not. Learning that is crucial to your decision-making process for the rest of the hand, and sometimes you have to pay heavily for the information! Another great thing about using a raise or reraise on the flop is that even though your purpose in betting was to find out if you had the best hand, your aggressive betting often causes a better hand to fold. Aggressive play in Hold'em is often rewarded in ways you weren't anticipating at the time; this is one of the reasons why jackals have developed their particular playing style, and why they seem to win more often than they should.

After all, most of the time the flop that you are hoping for in Hold'em just isn't there. When I make it three bets to go in a Hold'em hand with K-K, I'm hoping that no ace will hit the flop! And yet an ace does fall on the flop roughly 30 percent of the time. When I have Q-Q in a big multiway pot (with two or more opponents), then I'm hoping for neither an ace nor a king on the flop, because an ace or a king on the flop is the most likely way for me to lose the pot (to someone holding A-K or something similar). Yet often the ace or the king does come on the flop. But when you have Q-Q, and three small cards beneath the queen come on the flop, the hand is easy to play on the flop: just jam (raise and reraise) the pot!

I've been telling you to "ram and jam" (raise and reraise) with my top ten hands before the flop, but what happens when you've made it four bets to go with 10-10 and the flop comes 2-Q-K? This situation is a good bit trickier than one where you make it four bets to go with 10-10 and the flop comes down 10-7-2 (you have flopped the best possible hand in this case): there, you just jam it.

You'll be able to handle the dream flops, or even the really terrible flops, but what do you do when you're heavily involved in a hand before the flop but then have what for you is a marginal flop? What you do is raise your opponents as if you have hit the flop perfectly, and then watch to see how they react to your raises. If you get the strong impression that you're beaten, on the basis of your opponents' reactions to your raises, then fold. But if you're pretty sure you still have the best hand, then keep on betting or calling.

Notice here that woven into the principle of using raises on the flop to gain information about hands is the idea of using the occasion to read your opponents. I don't want to be teaching you just plain old boring game theory without also showing you how to take into account your opponents' moves, tendencies, and expressions. Poker is a lot more about reading your opponents than it is about how to play pocket eights against four opponents! If you do learn how to read someone, then everything will fall into place as you read this book. But if you don't know how to read someone (or think you don't), don't despair: reading people is also a skill that can be learned.

Now that I've shown you some of the power of the raise on the flop, I'm going to walk you through some examples that will help you learn how to play hands *after* the flop. But before I introduce these examples, I think it will be useful to tell a little story about a hand that I played at Foxwoods Casino (in Connecticut) in late 2001 during a $2,500-buy-in "World Poker Finals" Hold'em event. We were playing $300–$600 limit Hold'em when the following hand came up. I sat in the big blind, and three people called the $300 bet before the flop. Because I held 8-8, I raised, making it two bets, or $600, to go. My three opponents all called my raise, and the flop then came down A-9-5. I bet out $300, and everyone folded! This was terrific news for me, since most of the time in a big-buy-in poker event someone would have an ace in this situation. Four people times $600 each equals $2,400. I won $2,400 because I'd made the right bet on the flop and the right raise before the flop! If I hadn't bet on the flop, but had just checked, I probably would have lost this pot.

A lot of world-class players wouldn't have raised

before the flop on this hand, and therefore would have missed out on the extra $900 that I got the others to put into this pot before the flop. Some other strong players wouldn't have bet on the flop either, figuring that someone had to have an ace! I assumed or gambled (hoped) that my opponents had cards like K-10, Q-J, or 10c-8c, and for a $300 bet on the flop I earned $2,400.

If I had simply checked on the flop, rather than betting, then someone else might have tried to bluff, and I would have had a tough call, since I couldn't beat a pair of nines or aces. If I had checked and everyone had checked behind me, and then a king, queen, jack, or ten had come off on the turn, then I would probably have been beaten and would not have wanted to call a bet! Through playing this hand properly and making the bet on the flop, I won a pot that many players would not have won. Andy Glazer would have said this is a "Smith Barney pot," in the sense that I got my money the old-fashioned way: I earrrnnned it!

This is the principle I'm trying to illustrate, the principle of betting or raising on the flop, when you have a top ten hand, to find out if yours is the best hand. In this case I was representing an ace with my bet, and fortunately no one had an ace or a nine. If someone had raised me on this hand after I'd bet my

8-8 on the flop, then I most likely would have had to fold my hand, but the $300 bet was going to give me some valuable information, or at least a better chance of winning the pot (if it drove out someone who held something like K-Q and who might have caught that king or queen on the turn or the river), or, as wound up happening here, the whole pot.

Although I won the battle in this hand, I ended up losing the war in this particular tournament, going on to finish in twentieth place in a field of 100. Unfortunately for me on this day, poker tournaments usually conclude by paying only one table per hundred players, and here it was only the final table of nine players who "cashed."

EXAMPLES

Now let's take a look at the examples I've promised, situations that will teach you how to play your top ten hands after the flop. Seven assumptions will apply to the four examples that follow:

1. You're playing a $5–$10 online game at UltimateBet.com.
2. You have J-J, also known as pocket jacks.
3. Jim (a jackal) raises before the flop in the first position (the first player to act after the blinds,

usually referred to as "under the gun").
4. You reraise, making it three bets ($15) with your J-J in the third position.
5. Dumbo (an elephant) calls on the button.
6. Jerry (unclear profile) calls in the big blind.
7. Jim (the jackal) calls your raise.

The Flop Comes Down 10d-7d-4s

Jerry checks and Jim bets out $5. This is a very good flop for you, because there are no "overcards" (Q-K-A) to your pair of jacks (an overcard creates a reasonable possibility of a pair for someone who entered the pot with two big cards in his hand), and therefore there is an excellent chance that you still have the best hand.

Clearly, a raise is in order here. You raise because you probably have the best hand at this point, but your hand is vulnerable to overcards, and you want to try to drive out (force the player to fold) a hand like Q-K that can hit a queen or a king on either of the next two cards, and thus beat you. Your raise may also drive out someone with 5-5, who would otherwise call for the relatively cheap $5 and perhaps end up beating you because he hit a five on the next card or caught a six and then a three to make a straight. In other words, right now your raise is all about "protecting" your hand from losing by driving out opponents who, though trailing at the moment, have reasonable chances to beat you on the turn or river, if you let them stay in the hand. Your raise makes it too expensive for players facing weak draws to stay in the hand.

The Flop Has Come Down Ad-10s-4d

Jerry bets out and Jim calls. Now what do you do? A raise at this point is a great idea. Clearly, you cannot fold right here, because the pot is fairly large and you may still have the best hand. As long as you're going to play, you might as well raise it and find out if you have the best hand. You already know that you probably have Jim beat, because he's a jackal who always raises when he has any kind of hand and he didn't raise Jerry's $5 bet.

Assuming that you do raise, if Jerry reraises you here, he probably has you beat, but it's not a certainty: he could have a hand like a pair-and-a-flush draw, such as 10d-Qd, or a straight-and-a-flush draw with a hand like Qd-Kd. You should call his reraise on the flop, since it is only $5 more to you, and you want to see what he does after the next card is turned. If Jerry then bets out after the next card, where the limits are now doubled (he can bet $10 now and on the last round of betting), then it is time for a decision. You have to analyze what kind of hand Jerry is likely to have.

Does he have a drawing hand that you can beat or a hand like A-Q (a pair of aces; remember the flop is A-10-4) that beats you? Did the flush card or a king or queen hit the board on the turn? (Note, by the way, that even though a jack on the turn would appear to be a great card for you, because it would give you three jacks, it could also present some danger, if it is the jack of diamonds, or if someone had K-Q and has now made his straight.) If so, then can you beat anything anymore? Perhaps a "blank" card (a harmless card that helps neither a straight draw nor a flush draw) like the 6c comes off and Jerry checks his drawing hand to you. Why has he checked? Because your raise on the flop scared him off from betting the 6c. (If so, then your raise on the flop has accomplished its mission!) If he does bet here after a "blank," then you must watch the way he makes the bet (look for body language that might show confidence or fear) and make your best decision.

On fourth street (after the fourth up card is dealt), if something in your head (intuition or instinct) tells you that Jerry is bluffing, then call. If you feel that he has a real hand, then fold. Trust your instincts and you will find that they keep improving as you continue to play Hold'em.

You will also find that your ability to read others will get better as you gain experience, especially if you work specifically on watching how people bet their hands. One of the best times to do this is when you have folded your own hand and so no longer have to concentrate on your own tactical considerations: you can focus entirely on studying your opponents (and the outcome!) for information that will come in handy later.

The Flop Is Ac-Kd-4s

Jerry bets out $5, and Jim raises it to $10 to go. In this case there is no flush draw, and it's hard to imagine that both of your opponents have a straight draw with a hand like Q-J, Q-10, or J-10. Although one of your opponents might have a hand like that, what does the other one have? Almost certainly the other opponent has a pair of kings or a pair of aces, because people holding high-rank cards like that tend to stay in hands. In this case, the two overcards on the flop make folding your hand an easy choice. This is one of the worst possible flops for a pair of jacks, especially in a three-bet pot where your opponents probably hold A-something or K-Q, K-J, or K-10.

"But wait a minute," you might ask; "if my opponent can get lucky by hitting the ace he was drawing to on the flop, why can't I get lucky and hit a jack on the turn or the river?" If one of your opponents does have a pair of aces or kings, then you can win only by hitting a jack (don't even factor in the extremely unlikely chance of hitting two perfect cards in a row to make a straight); and because there are only two jacks left in the deck, the odds against that happening are about 22-to-1 on the next card. Just say to yourself, "OK, I've played this hand perfectly so far, so even though I've waited a long time for a pair of jacks, it's time to fold them. Next time I have a big hand, I hope I draw a better flop to it." Then simply fold your hand and forget about the outcome of that one. (But again, see what the outcome tells you about Jerry or Jim.)

Of course, the jack sometimes hits right away, and sometimes you would have won the pot because your opponents have Q-10 and 4d-Qd. (Obviously the jackal has this hand!) But regardless of the outcome, you will have made the right move by folding. Sometimes people drive themselves crazy by second-guessing their plays. The next thing you know they're staying in pots trying to hit the shots that are 22-to-1 against them, and virtually giving their money away! Sometimes poker will drive you batty or, in poker terms, put you "on tilt."

If you can keep your emotions in check when

bad luck smacks you hard—if you can avoid letting a bad break in one hand affect the way you play your next hand—you will have an excellent chance to become a winning poker player. But if you find that you can't get the last hand out of your mind, and you're vulnerable to tilt, you will probably find it impossible to win over the long haul. In the long run, I'd rather invest my money in a "good" player who never goes on tilt than in a "very good" player who is vulnerable to going on tilt.

The Flop Is Kd-Qd-7s

Jerry checks, and Jim bets out $5. A lot of us would be tempted to think, "OK, I'm probably beaten in this hand because I cannot beat someone who has a king or a queen in his hand and I'm facing three opponents in this pot. But I'm not convinced yet that I'm beat, so I'll just call the $5." In fact, a "mouse" might even fold his hand at this point! But this is the wrong way to look at it. Yes, you probably are beaten, but for an extra $5 (raising instead of calling) you can gain a lot of information, and because of your raise you might even win this pot. Assuming that you do make the correct raise, making it $10 to go, you might:

1. Have Jim the jackal beaten and force Dumbo to fold his Q-J (even though it has you beat

with a pair of queens, Dumbo will be afraid you have a king in your hand). This is an example of winning a pot through aggressive play. The beautiful thing about this scenario is that you were really just making a raise to gain information about the strength of your hand, but as a by-product you forced the best hand to fold!

2. Have Jim the jackal beaten and force Dumbo to fold his A-10, a hand he might have played for $5 trying to hit an inside straight, and lo and behold, the play saves you a fortune when your third jack comes off on the next card, because it would have given Dumbo an ace-high straight (10-J-Q-K-A)!

3. Find out that Dumbo has you beaten when he reraises the pot behind you, making it $15 to go. Now you can call $5 more on the outside chance that a jack will hit the board or that Dumbo is sitting on a big draw like Ad-Jd and will check it on the next two streets if he misses his hand. But if he bets again or if Jim calls the $15 total on the flop, you will have to fold. At least you will know that you are beaten at this point in the hand, and you can avoid calling the next two $10 bets.

4. Find out that you are beaten because all three

of your opponents called your $10 bet on the flop, and it's just too unreasonable to think that your pair of jacks is the best hand after they all call a bet and a raise. (All three would have to be on either a smaller pair than jacks, or a straight draw, or the flush draw, and this is pretty unlikely.)

5. Eliminate all the other opponents in the hand, but find that Jim does have you beat. In this case, you will probably wind up losing some extra bets to Jim because he's a jackal! This is an example of what I mentioned earlier—of how jackals don't lose as much as their wild play would seem to indicate, because they get paid off big-time when they actually do make a strong hand. But you will have ample opportunity to get those bets back from Jim later on, in another hand!

You can now see why raising Jim's bet here on the flop may win the pot for you, or at least give you the additional information that says your hand is beaten. Of your three options, raising is best, folding is second best, and calling is the worst! Your raise on the flop will set up the way you play your hand on the next two rounds of betting, and it may bluff out a better hand.

PLAYING THE FLOP, FOR LIMIT HOLD'EM BEGINNERS: THE SPECIAL CASE OF A-K

It's time now to tackle an old problem in the Texas Hold'em game: how to play A-K after a bad flop. Since you will be putting in a lot of bets before the flop with A-K, you can usually play this hand pretty aggressively after the flop as well (because you've already built a pretty good-size pot, one worth going after).

Even though we are only in the beginners' section for limit Hold'em, I want to talk briefly here about the historical significance of A-K in no-limit Hold'em tournaments. The classic hand to come up between two players in big no-limit Hold'em tournaments is A-K versus Q-Q. Many times one of these tournaments is decided because a great player has hit or missed his A-K versus Q-Q for a mountain of chips! At the 2001 World Series of Poker, which is the poker world's world championships, I had Q-Q early in one event and was "all-in" (all my remaining chips were in the pot) against my opponent's A-K. I put my last $2,000 in before the flop with my Q-Q, and my opponent called me with A-K. If I had lost this "coin flip" (actually, Q-Q is about a 13-to-10 favorite), then I would have been eliminated and would not have gone on to win the event and $305,000 for first place. This is a fairly common occurrence late in these events. It makes sense, considering that the hands J-J, Q-Q, K-K, A-A, and A-K are the top five hands in Hold'em. The trick is to "finish the job" and go on to win the event if you are lucky enough to win a big coin-flip pot.

EXAMPLES

Now that I've shown you the key role that A-K often plays in no-limit Hold'em events, it's time to set up the next five examples. Here are your six assumptions:

1. You have A-K in the small blind in a $2–$4 game at your house (someone may win or lose up to $200, but usually $50–$100 wins and losses are to be expected at this limit).
2. A jackal named Joe makes it $4 to go in the third position.
3. An elephant named Earl calls the $4 on the button.
4. You reraise, making it $6 to go from the small blind.

5. The big-blind lion named Leo calls the $6 bet.

6. Joe the jackal and Earl the elephant also call the $6 bet.

The Flop Includes an Ace or a King (for Example, A-9-4, K-10-7, A-2-3, or K-Q-J)

You bet, raise, and reraise quite a bit because you have hit "top pair" with "top kicker." In every case where an ace or a king hits the flop you will have top pair with top kicker (A-A-K or A-K-K), and this is a very strong hand in Hold'em! For example, if the flop is A-9-4, then you have a pair of aces with a king kicker. This hand will beat all other pairs of aces like A-Q, A-J, A-10, A-8, etc.

But let's suppose now that the flop is A-9-4 and someone is holding A-9. Your A-K would be losing on this flop, because A-9 now makes two pair, aces and nines. Still, for every time someone who plays a weak A-9 against your powerful A-K and beats you, you'll beat him more than two other times (that is, the A-K is slightly more than a 2.5-to-1 favorite heads-up against A-9). The point I'm trying to make is that A-K becomes very powerful when you catch an ace or a king on the flop, and you should put in a lot of betting and raising on the flop when this is the case. Fortunes have been won and lost with A-K!

Now let's move on to a few examples of how to play the A-K when you miss the flop.

The Flop Is J-5-2

You bet out $2. The lion, Leo, raises, making it $4 to go; and the elephant, Earl, calls the bet. In this case you figure that one of your opponents has you beat, but you call $2 anyway, on the chance that an ace, king, queen, or ten will hit the board on fourth street. If an ace or king hits, then you should bet out $4 on fourth street. But if a queen or ten hits, then you will want to call a $4 bet (check and then call $4 if your opponents bet) because you have picked up a straight draw. Since you know you will call $4 when a queen or a ten hits, you may choose to bet out $4, attempting to win the pot right there (but right now we are talking about play on the flop). So the play on the flop here is fairly simple: you bet out $2 and call the raise of $2.

The Flop Is 7d-8d-9d and You Have As-Kc

You bet out $2, and the lion raises it to $4 to go. The jackal calls $4. Now what do you do? Folding here isn't a bad option, because two of the cards that under other conditions you would like to see on the turn or river, Ad or Kd, would make four diamonds on the board, so they're very likely good cards for someone else, bad cards for you. Still, it costs you only $2 to see if you can hit your hand. I would probably just fold for $2, but an expert could call the $2 bet, because he feels that he reads his opponents well enough to avoid getting too involved later on in the hand. The point I'm trying to make is this: sometimes, even though you have A-K, you have to fold your hand on the flop when the others raise you. You're not folding often, mind you, but situations where you face three suited connected cards like 7d-8d-9d or 8h-9h-10h on the board, and you have none of the suited cards in your hand (like with As-Ks), are just too likely to have helped someone else in the hand. Those two examples are the worst possible flops for your As-Kc, and it's probably right to just fold your hand on the spot.

The Flop Is Q-10-2

You bet out $2, the lion raises it to $4, and then the elephant reraises it to $6 to go. In this case, you need a jack for a straight or an ace or a king for a pair. You have to call the $6. You have to figure that at least one of your opponents has you beaten, even though one of them may have a hand like K-J, an open-ended straight draw. (You may even consider raising it again to make it $8 to go! Whoops, never mind, that's a play for the advanced discussion, still to come.) The point of this example is that if what turns up on the flop gives you a straight draw, then you need to play your A-K. Three available aces, three available kings, and four of whatever card completes your straight draw (in this case four jacks) give you too many winning possibilities (pros call this having ten "outs") to fold right away.

The Flop Is 6-5-2

You bet out $2, and the lion calls. Then the jackal makes it $4 to go, and the elephant folds. What do you do now? You probably have the lion beaten, since he only called the $2 on the flop, and lions usually don't merely call when they're pretty sure they have the best of it. The jackal could easily have you beaten with a pair of deuces, fives, or sixes, and jackals play a lot of strange hands. But he is the jackal and he could just as easily have 7-8, A-4, A-3, 7-9, or 8-9, all of which give him a straight draw of one sort or another. If this is the case, then you are a favorite over his hand. (He has to hit something with only two cards to go, while you're already winning and don't need to improve to beat him.) You're going to call the $2 raise anyway, so why not reraise, making it $6 to go?

The reraise will probably cause the lion to fold his hand, isolating you (getting it down to just the two of you) against the jackal. If you don't reraise, and the jackal does have 8-9, and the lion does have Qd-Jd, you might end up losing the hand to the lion because you let him in cheap! This is the advantage of being the jackal; his erratic play sometimes causes you to put in extra bets against him. But aggressive play against the jackal is a good thing! Since he will play his drawing hands "fast" (raising and reraising), you will have a chance to win some big pots when he misses his hand. What I'm really trying to say is this: play your "A-K high" (the best nonpair hand) aggressively on the flop against the jackal when you think there is a decent chance he's drawing. You can always fold your hand on fourth street or the river if you think the jackal has you beat.

We'll talk more about how to play A-K on the flop in the intermediate discussion of limit Hold'em, to come.

HOW TO PLAY THE TOP TEN HANDS ON FOURTH STREET

One great benefit of the style that I'm teaching you to use in Texas Hold'em is that fourth street and the river are now easier to play, because you will have done some good work on the flop (raising) to find out whether or not you have the best hand. Fourth street is the time for you to use the information you've learned on the flop. Because the bets are now doubled on this round of betting, a well-timed fold will save you at least two big bets, perhaps more. On the other hand, a well-timed raise may win the whole pot for you! If you believe you have the best hand after the fourth card is turned up, then you need to make a bet or a raise. If you've learned that you are beaten, now is the time to fold your hand.

First, let's take a look at some obvious plays (obvious to an expert, at least) and how they may affect the outcome of a hand.

Protecting Your Hand
You have K-K. A jackal raises before the flop, you then make it three bets (reraise), and an elephant behind you calls the three bets "cold" (without

having any money already invested in the pot). The jackal then calls the one additional bet.

The flop comes 10-9-2 and the jackal bets, you raise, and the elephant calls the two bets. The jackal also calls two bets. The turn card comes up a two, for 10-9-2-2, and now the jackal bets out into you. At this point you should be thinking, "Raise it!" But you're distracted by the conversation going on across the table, and you just call the bet. Now, the elephant calls the bet as well.

This is a most costly mistake, since you've now let the elephant call only one bet with his A-9, and the last card off is an ace, for 10-9-2-2-A. Now the jackal checks and you decide to check as well, because you fear the ace may have hit the elephant. Then the elephant bets and the jackal calls, and you call as well. The elephant then says, "I have two pair, aces up." You think, "Man, am I unlucky, I cannot believe that he hit an ace on me here!" Wrong! You misplayed this hand! All you had to do was raise after the two came up on fourth street, and the elephant would have been forced to throw his hand away! Your call on the end might also fall into the mistake category (even though I've said you should generally not be folding on the end), because the one card you had legitimate reason to fear, the ace, hit the board, and a bet and a call were already in front of you.

Let's rewrite the script, then, so you're making the obvious raise on fourth street. A deuce comes off the deck for 10-9-2-2, and the jackal bets out into you. You don't really think the jackal has a deuce, so you raise and the elephant reluctantly folds his hand. The jackal calls your raise. The river card is an ace, for 10-9-2-2-A, and the jackal checks. You conclude that the jackal has a pair of tens, so you bet out, and then the jackal calls you. You say, "Pocket kings for me" and the jackal says, "Nice hand." You then pile all the chips onto your stack as the elephant loudly complains, "Darn it, I would have made aces and nines if I'd stayed in, but I couldn't call, because your raise on fourth street told me you had me beaten!" You just smile and finish stacking the chips, thinking, "Looks as though I played that hand perfectly!"

This first example is about "protecting your hand" with a raise on fourth street. If you fail to do that, you give your opponents a chance to outdraw you for just one bet. The next example is another fairly obvious play, but in the other direction—folding!

Knowing When to Fold 'Em
Two opponents have called the bet before the flop,

and now you make it two bets to go with Jc-Js on the button. The big blind and both other opponents call the raise, and the flop comes 2d-3d-Qs. The big blind checks, the first "limper" (caller) bets out, and the second limper folds. You then raise to find out "where you're at" (great strategy!) and the big blind calls. The remaining limper, whose play falls somewhere between that of a lion and that of a jackal (he's a fairly strong player who's sometimes unpredictable), now reraises, making it three bets to go. You call, and now the big blind calls as well.

Fourth street brings 4d, for 2d-3d-Qs-4d, and the big blind checks and the limper bets out. You fold because you can't beat a pair of queens or a flush (the flush draw hit!) and you're afraid of both the limper and the big blind. What hand could the limper make it three bets with on the flop, and nonetheless be a hand you can now beat?

If he has a flush draw, then he hits his flush. If he has a pair of queens, then you're already beat. If he has a "set" (trips made with a pocket pair like 2-2 and a two on the board), then you're also beat. Of course it's possible that the limper is overplaying a pair of threes, like A-3 (with 2-3-Q on board) or something similar, but it's very unlikely that he would reraise on the flop with that hand. About the only realistic hope for you is that the limper three-bet with A-K, a hand your jacks still beat. That's certainly not an impossible holding, but are you willing to pay off big bets on both the turn and the river to find out if you're right? If the limper is willing to push A-K on the turn, there's a very realistic possibility that he will push one more time with it on the river. I won't carry the script of this hand further, but suffice to say that you made the right play, because there is almost no hand that you can beat at this point in the hand. Chasing (calling) on the strength of the slight hope that the limper is playing like a maniac and pushing his A-K will gouge big chunks out of your bankroll over the long run.

Folding Down Your Hand

With a hand of 10-10 you've made it three bets to go over the top of a lion before the flop, and two other opponents have called. This means you have four players putting in three bets each. The flop comes up Ac-4d-5s, the lion bets, and you raise him, but this time he reraises you (assume that everyone else folds on the flop).

Fourth street is the time to fold this hand. The lion can't be drawing here, because there is no draw, and you can assume the lion isn't playing 6-7!

The jackal might have 6-7, but the lion wouldn't.
So when the lion bets out again, into you, after the
9d comes up, for Ac-4d-5s-9d, it's time to fold your
hand. The lion's response to your raise on the flop
lets you know that he has you beaten! Now act on
the information you've paid for, and fold your
hand. You may even want to show the lion your
hand and say, "OK, you win because I fold."
Although you are giving away free information
when you show your hand in this spot, sometimes
this sort of ad hoc play encourages your opponent
to show you his hand for free (now or in some later
hand), and you may wind up collecting a lot more
free information than you've given away.

EXAMPLES

Let's now revisit an example we looked at earlier
and consider a few different possibilities.

Ten assumptions for the following five examples:

1. The game is $5–$10 at UltimateBet.com.
2. You have Jc-Js (pocket jacks).
3. Jim (a jackal) raises before the flop in the first
   position.
4. You make it three bets ($15) with J-J in the
   third position.

5. Dumbo (an elephant) calls on the button.
6. Jerry (unclear profile) calls in the big blind.
7. Jim calls your raise.
8. The flop comes down Ad-10s-4d.
9. Jerry bets out and Jim calls the bet.
10. You raise with your Jc-Js, making it two bets to go.

Folding Your Hand Because a Bad Card Has Come on Fourth Street

Jerry makes it three bets, and Jim calls three bets. Now you call three bets, but you now believe that Jerry has some kind of a strong hand. You aren't sure if Jerry has an ace, or a flush draw *and* a straight draw (like Kd-Qd, Kd-Jd, or Qd-Jd), or a flush draw and a pair like 10d-Qd, 10d-Kd, or 10d-xd (x is a random card). The next card is the 6d, for Ad-10s-4d-6d, and Jerry bets out into you and Jim folds. OK, the flush draw has hit, so you fold your hand, because you figure that Jerry has either an ace or a flush.

Protecting Your Hand

Jerry and Jim both call your raise, and the next card off the deck is the 8s, for Ad-10s-4d-8s. Jerry and Jim now check to you. They probably aren't

checking an ace (a pair of aces) to you, and you
don't want to give them a free draw at their flush,
or at an overcard hand like K-Q. So you bet to protect your hand.

The Elephant Scares You Off

Dumbo makes it three bets to go, and he isn't the
type to raise it unless he has a big hand. Dumbo
makes a lot of calls but doesn't raise too often. Jerry
now folds, and Jim calls the $15 bet. It is only $5
more to you to call, so I would call, but I'd be
ready to fold my hand on fourth street for one bet
from Dumbo. I would be thinking that Dumbo
has at least a pair of aces with a high kicker, and
probably two pair, aces up with A-10 or A-6.

Raising the Jackal on Fourth Street
When a Good Card Hits

Jerry and Jim both call your raise on the flop, and
now the As comes off the deck for Ad-10s-4d-As.
(This is a good card for you: first, because now
there are only two aces left and the chances that
one of your two opponents has it are decreased;
second, because this isn't a straight or a flush card.)
Jerry checks and now Jim bets out into you. You
decide that you have Jim beat and you raise to protect your hand, because there is a chance that your

raise here will cause Jerry to fold his flush draw. If Jerry does have an ace, you will know when he raises it to $30 to go, and now you can fold your hand. Either way, you're pretty sure you have Jim beaten here, because he's a jackal who hasn't made a bet or raise until now! Don't be afraid to raise Jim on fourth street if you think you have him beat.

A Tough Situation

Jerry reraises you on the flop, making it three bets, and Jim calls the three bets. You also call the three bets. Now 6s comes off the deck, for Ad-10s-4d-6s, Jerry bets out into you, and Jim calls the bet. Now you have a tough situation to deal with! You really aren't worried that Jim might have you beaten. The question is, does Jerry have you beat (as he would with an ace or three fours) or is he holding a big draw like 10d-Qd, 10d-9d, Jd-Qd, Qd-Kd, or something similar? I would lean toward folding my hand here, but everything would depend on my read of the player. Is Jerry the type to try to bluff me here? When I look straight at him, what do I sense he is pondering? Does he want me to call or to fold right now? Just make your best guess and go with it! You will find that the more often you're put in this situation, the better you become at reading your opponents.

PLAYING THE RIVER WITH THE TOP TEN HANDS: CALL FOR THE POT ODDS!

In general, if you've made it all the way to the river with your top ten hand, then it's probably correct to call one bet on the river. The concept of "pot odds" will help me explain to you why I like to make a lot of calls on the river in Hold'em. In poker slang, I'm a "calling station" on the river in limit Hold'em; I'm from Missouri, the "Show me" state!

If the game is $5–$10, and I've played my top ten hand aggressively throughout the pot, then the amount of money already in the pot might be $140. For example, I make it $15 to go with three opponents ($60) before the flop, and now I raise on the flop and two opponents call my raise ($30). Then I bet out and two opponents call my bet on fourth street ($30), and finally one opponent bets out into me and my other opponent calls ($20). So the pot holds $60 + $30 + $30 + $20 = $140. Now, my $10 call gives me a chance to win $140!

If you do decide to fold here, then you must be at least 93 percent sure that you are beat (10/140 = 0.0714, and 1 - .0714 = .9286). That's why I don't lay down too many hands on the river! Of course, when the worst possible card for my hand hits on the river and a mouse bets into me, then I'm 98 percent sure that I'm beaten! So the $140 pot is laying me 14-to-1 odds on my call. $140 to $10 is pretty strong pot odds! This is why I encourage being a calling station like me in limit Hold'em!

EXAMPLES

Having said all that, I'll start with two examples of where I would fold a hand, even on the river.

Folding on the River

Let's assume that you have Q-Q in a four-way-action pot with a board of 5d-10d-Js-7s, and that there has been a lot of betting and raising on the flop during this hand. Say now that Ad comes off the deck and a mouse bets into you. You'll want to fold your hand without further thought. The Ad makes a flush, a straight, and a pair of aces all possible. That combined with the specter of a mouse betting into you is a scary scenario! You'd probably have to fold even if a jackal bet into you, especially if there are other opponents in the hand behind you yet to act. It is also a bad sign for you that there was so much betting and raising on the flop; this suggests that there are straight and flush draws out there. Some cards are just so bad that you have to fold.

The Board Is So Bad I Surrender!

Suppose you have As-Ad, the flop comes 8h-9h-10h (this is one of the worst possible flops for your hand), and two opponents are really "jamming it" with you on the flop. Say 2c hits on the turn, they both check, you bet, and they both call you. Now you know that you probably have the best hand at this point, since no one has raised you, but you're also sure that your opponents have big draws. (What else could they have been jamming it with on the flop?) So when Jh pops up on the river, for 8h-9h-10h-2c-Jh, what can you beat? Any heart makes a flush and any seven or queen makes a straight. How can you call even one bet on the end, especially given the way the others have played the hand? You can't even beat an opponent who holds 10c-Jc (that hand makes two pairs). Even though you waited hours for your A-A, and even though the pot odds are pretty good, sometimes you just have to surrender!

Now let's take a look at some situations where, most of the time, you just have to call on the river because of the pot odds.

A Hand with Three Different Endings

Here's a familiar situation, involving Jim (the jackal) and Jerry (unknown profile). You have J-J and you've made it three bets over the top of Jim's two bets (reraised) before the flop. Jerry calls you from the big blind, and the flop is Ad-10s-4d. Jerry bets out on the flop, Jim calls the bet, and you raise it, to find out what they really have. Both players call your raise, and then 6s comes off on the turn and they both check to you. You bet out, thinking your J-J is still the best hand, and they both call again.

The last card is Kd, for a final board of Ad-10s-4d-6s-Kd. Jerry bets out and Jim calls. The Kd was probably the worst possible card for your hand, other than 10d, because now you can't beat a flush, a straight, or a pair of kings. Jerry probably has you beaten, but how about Jim? It looks to me as if Jim has you beaten here as well.

Here, I'd put Jim on K-Q, which makes a pair of kings for him on the end. Think about it. If Jim has a flush, then he would have raised on the end. If Jim has kings and tens (another possibility, given the way the hand unfolded), then he would probably have raised on the flop himself, with his pair of tens. Whatever the case may be, it looks as if Jim has you beaten. It's true that there is already

$125 ($45 + $30 + $30 + $20) in the pot, so you need to be over 92 percent sure that you're beaten before you decide to fold. But given this situation, I would have to fold, because I'd be convinced that both players have me beaten. Both players expect you to call on the end, and the chances that both of them are trying to bluff you therefore seem very remote.

Let's suppose now that the last card is 6c, for Ad-10s-4d-6s-6c, and now Jerry bets out into you and Jim folds. This bet would seem very suspicious to me, and I would call it very quickly. I would be thinking, "Why did Jerry decide to bet right here and now? I don't think that the six helped him, so he's either bluffing or holding an ace." If I'm facing an either-or situation and getting this kind of pot odds, I'm going to call without hesitation.

Let's suppose again that the last card is 6c, for Ad-10s-4d-6s-6c, and now both opponents check to you. Do you bet here or check? If you bet here, you have to be hoping that either Jerry or Jim will call you with a pair of tens or worse. I wouldn't be worried about Jim in this case, but Jerry would concern me a little bit. (Could Jerry have an ace with no kicker, like A-2, A-3, or A-5, which would explain why he just called on the flop? Did he fear an ace with a kicker on the flop?) This "value bet" that you're considering making (a bet you make believing that it will earn slightly more than it will lose, over the long run) is one that needs a little bit of reading ability as well (a little finesse). If you decide to bet, then that's fine; if you decide to check, that's fine too. I would bet it myself unless I felt strongly that Jerry had me beaten. We'll talk more about value betting in the intermediate and advanced sections.

Pot Odds Say, "Close Your Eyes and Call"

You're holding K-K, and you three-bet an elephant before the flop. The flop then comes down 5d-6s-7h, and now you make it four bets (a raising war on the flop). The next card off is 10s and he checks and then calls your bet. Now 8s comes off on the river, for 5d-6s-7h-10s-8s, and the elephant bets out into you. In this case, any four or nine makes a straight, but you call the bet quickly because you can still beat a lot of hands. The pot odds are heavily in your favor for a call here—there is already $7 from the blinds that folded, $30 from before the flop, $40 on the flop, $20 from fourth street, and $10 from the elephant's bet on the end. One $10 call to win $107! I'd call quickly as well.

Suppose it's Ad that comes off on the river, for

5d-6s-7h-10s-Ad, and the elephant bets out into you. I'd call quickly here as well, because of the pot odds (there is a lot of money in this pot).

Calling Two Bets on the River

The question here is whether or not you should call on the river when calling costs you two big bets. In general, when you have to call two bets (someone bets and then someone else raises) on the river in a Hold'em pot, it's a good idea to fold. Usually, the only hands that you can beat on the end, when it costs you two bets just to call, are bluffs. You will rarely see an experienced player bluff raise on the river in low-limit Hold'em! It's just not a very profitable play. To return to a familiar example: let's assume that the hand has been played out among Jim, Jerry, and you, as detailed above. When Jerry bets out into Ad-10s-4d-6s-Kd and Jim raises, it's a good idea to exit stage left with your modest little J-J.

If the last card is 6c, leaving Ad-10s-4d-6s-6c, and, as before, Jerry bets out and Jim raises, then get out of that one too. Even though 6c seems a harmless card, all you can really beat here is a bluff by both players. Is it really possible that both Jerry and Jim are bluffing? I don't think so! (If you want another reason to fold this hand, suppose now that you call, and Jerry really has the goods, something like A-6, and reraises! Now what are you going to do?)

Folding A-A for Two Bets on the End

When John bets out into 5d-6d-8c-10s-4d on the end and Frank raises to two bets, then it's a good time to dump your A-A even though the pot is huge! When they bet and raise at this point in the hand, what can you beat? It seems likely that one of your opponents has made a flush or a straight (he needs to have only a seven in his hand for a straight) or at least two pair. I'm assuming in this example that you played your A-A very aggressively and put in a lot of bets, which would have discouraged them from thinking that they could bluff you on the river.

When the Last Card Is Bad for Your Hand

Let's assume that you have put in a lot of bets with your Q-Q (pocket queens), that two opponents have called, and that the board has developed 4c-5c-9h-Js on the turn. Let's consider two scenarios.

In the first scenario, both opponents have just called you on fourth street and now the last card is 9c, for a final board of 4c-5c-9h-Js-9c. Your first opponent then bets out into you, and now it's your turn to act, with your other opponent waiting behind you. Wow, what an awful card 9c was for your hand! You can't beat anyone who is holding either a nine (he now has *trips*, or three of a kind) or two clubs (he now has a flush), and either of those is a hand pretty likely to have withstood your heavy raising on the flop. A nine would have given him top pair on the flop, and the flop presented a flush draw.

I might lean toward folding here for the first bet (I would fold to a mouse, but not to a jackal), but let's assume that you call and now the opponent behind you raises and the other opponent calls. In this situation you can be almost certain you are beat. Judging from the fact that they have bet into you, raised you, and then called the raise, you can suppose they pretty much know your hand! (By the way, my guess here is that they both have your Q-Q beat.) Yikes, you had better fold, even though the pot odds are huge. The point is that you need to be very concerned when someone raises on the river! Ironically, the great size of the pot (which so powerfully entices you to call) demonstrates that they almost certainly have you beat, because they will have assumed you would call them with such a large pot staring you in the face. In very-high-stakes games, this isn't always going to be true, but when you're starting out, you aren't going to be seeing very many bluff raises on the river.

Let's assume now that 6c comes off on the river, for a final board of 4c-5c-9h-Js-6c, and that the first opponent bets out into you. The second opponent is sitting behind you, waiting for you to act. This card is bad for you, because it completes the flush draws, but not nearly as bad as the 9c we looked at in the preceding example, because it doesn't give trips to those folks who may have started with top pair. Here, you have to call your first opponent. But if the second opponent raises, then you have to fold, regardless of whether the first opponent called the second opponent's raise or not. It's just too hard for the second opponent to bluff here. What's he going to do, raise hoping that both of you will fold?

In general, when you aren't sure whether or not to call one bet on the river, then call. The pot odds support a whole lot of calling on the river, because in the long run you don't often have to be too successful in picking off a bluff for this call to prove profitable! Generally, though, I would fold my hand on the river for two bets, since rarely do you see someone making it two bets to go on the river on a bluff. Of course, if your instincts say fold, or call, or raise on the river, and you've begun to trust your instincts, then follow them!

So, before the flop in limit Hold'em, play only the top ten hands, and make sure that you play them very aggressively. On the flop, remember to raise to find out "where you're at" so that you can make the right moves later on in the hand or possibly win a pot through your aggressive play that others wouldn't have won. On fourth street, make sure that you protect your hand, or fold it, depending on what you learned on the flop, what card came off, and the way the betting came down. On the river, look to call down your opponents because of the pot-odds principle, but be leery of calling two bets on the river.

You've now learned enough to win money playing poker in most small-stakes games. Remember, though, that it may take a long time to digest all the information I've given you so far. Before you rush on out and play, keep in mind that you need to learn to walk before you can fly. You're not ready to play with Junior's graduation money just yet.

Four

LIMIT HOLD'EM: INTERMEDIATE STRATEGY

If you have a really steep learning curve, and the ability to read players well, then you may be able to move up rather quickly from the beginners' level to the next, intermediate level of limit Hold'em. But usually, in order to reach the intermediate level, you will need to play for at least a few months and absorb the nuances of limit Hold'em.

The intermediate-level limit Hold'em player does extremely well in low-limit games. In fact, he does so well that he wants to test himself at the next level up. For example, if you begin to beat your $2–$4 home poker game consistently, then it is time for you to try a higher-stakes home poker game (or casino game)—perhaps $4–$8 or $5–$10.

If you're only breaking even or losing at this higher level, then you need to drop back down and continue to win at the lower levels for a while before you test your game again. But if you're a good intermediate-level player and you do well in the $4–$8 games, then you will want to try playing $8–$16 or $10–$20 limit.

Every great player that I know of has moved up through the limits in this way, with some drop-offs along the way. You start out playing $1–$2 limit Hold'em with your friends, and the next thing you know, you're playing $400–$800 limit at the Bellagio with Phil Hellmuth, Johnny Chan, and Doyle Brunson! I personally won about $20,000 in home games in 1986, but when I stepped up to Las Vegas casino play, I slowly lost the whole $20,000 and went broke for the first and (so far!) last time. A bumpy road on the way up is to be expected—no one climbs Mount Everest with ease!

EXTENDING YOUR PLAY BEYOND THE TOP TEN HANDS

It's time to add a few more hands to the mix. I call the new group of hands the "majority play hands" because you can play all of them in the majority of the Hold'em games you find yourself in. Recall that the top ten hands in Chapter 3 were A-A, K-K, Q-Q, A-K, J-J, 10-10, 9-9, 8-8, A-Q, and 7-7. The majority play hands are 6-6, 5-5, 4-4, 3-3, 2-2, A-x suited, and K-Q. "A-x suited" simply means an ace and any other card of the same suit, like Ad-4d, Ac-5c, As-2s, Ah-3h, etc.

In this chapter you will learn:

➤ How to "steal the blinds."
➤ Phil's "majority play" hands.
➤ The "calling" theory on how to play small pairs.
➤ The "reraising" theory on how to play small pairs.
➤ How to play K-Q.
➤ How to "trap" players ("slow-playing" and "smooth-calling").

The intermediate-level majority-play-hands strategy will be more "swingy" than the top-ten-hands strategy. By swingy, I mean that you'll find that your chip stack goes up and down both more frequently and for higher amounts when you use this intermediate-play strategy along with the top-ten-hands strategy. For example, you may now lose a small pot or win a big pot when you play Ac-3c against your opponent's A-Q (most of the time you'll lose). Using just the top-ten-hands strategy, you would never have gotten involved in this hand, so your chip stack wouldn't have had to endure the swings up or down that this confrontation can create.

Similarly, you will lose many small pots when you play hands like 2-2 or 3-3, but you will also win some really big ones when you flop a set, the poker slang term for three of a kind. Of course, you're not guaranteed to win when you flop a set, but I like your chances! The problem is that you will flop a set only one time out of every $7\frac{1}{2}$ attempts. That's why playing this hand will cause you to lose a lot of small pots: most of the time you'll miss the flop, but you'll be smart enough to fold when you do, and when you do hit the flop, you'll probably score well.

STEALING THE BLINDS

We'll get into the play of these majority play hands soon, but first I need to introduce a strategy called "stealing the blinds," one that can yield a few chips in certain circumstances, even with a worthless hand, and at minimal risk. In most tough games, you'll see a lot of folding before the flop. When everyone folds up to the player on the button, then that player will usually raise in the hope that the small blind and big blind will fold their hands too. If they do, then the button player gets to keep the blind money. Even if the player on the button has something like 5-8, he will often raise in this situation in order to try to steal the blinds. Experienced opponents will know that the button player who raises at this point might be attempting to steal, but if their hands are just as bad, they'll fold rather than get involved with a bad hand in bad position. You can see how the term "stealing" would have arisen when players put in a raise with a hand this weak!

The power of the blind steal is related to the fact that the button player has the best position. Being on the button gives a player the advantage of position, in that he will act last during the whole hand. In Hold'em, acting last (having position) is a huge edge. If you're powerful, weak, or somewhere in between, you can sit back and wait for all the other players to reveal their strength or weakness before you act on your hand. Two good reasons for you to fold a marginal hand in the blinds when the button raises are that you're in bad position and that the button may actually have a real hand instead of a weak hand.

Weird Things Can Happen When You're Stealing the Blinds

I still remember a hand that came up with 11 players left (five at one table and six at my table) in a limit Hold'em event at Caesar's Palace in 1991. With the limits at $1,000–$2,000 I decided to raise in late position with Qd-7s. The poker legend Hans "Tuna" Lund (twice a final-table finisher at the World Series of Poker!) decided to call me with 10-J in the big blind, because he thought that I was just trying to steal his blind.

The flop came up Q-10-7, which gave me a very powerful two pair, and Tuna checked and then called my $1,000 bet. When a jack came off on fourth street, giving him two pair (tens and jacks), he bet out $2,000 and I raised him to $4,000. He then reraised me, and I just called his three bets ($6,000), thinking that he probably had me beat. Tuna then bet out $2,000 on the end, and I called. He then stated, "Two pair, jacks up," and I responded, "No good, I have queens up." Tuna replied, "You lucky puppy, I knew you were just trying to steal the blinds!"

It was indeed a very lucky hand to have come up with, when 11 players were left in the tournament and the limits were as high as they were. I won a

$22,500 pot all because I was trying to steal the blinds! Of course, although an attempt to steal may lead to either a successful steal with nothing or a big win like the one I got against Tuna, you can also end up losing a big pot if you flop something good in that endeavor and it loses to something better.

In another tournament, this one at the U.S. Poker Open at the Taj Mahal in Atlantic City in 1997, I kept trying to steal the blinds, and I kept getting crushed! I would steal from a position one off the button (you will observe that a steal attempt looks less like a steal attempt the farther you are from the button) with 9-10, and I'd get called with K-10. Then the old 10-4-2 flop would hit and I would lose the maximum. Or I would raise with 8d-9d stealing on the button and be called with Q-J. With a flop of J-10-2, I then had to play my open-ended straight draw all the way. And boom—an eight would come up on the last card and I would call that bet too! After repeatedly getting crushed stealing the blinds that day, I decided to be more careful in the future, both in using that play and in how aggressively I would continue on after I got called, and so should you. So again, blind-stealing can cut both ways. (It will crop up in various examples in this chapter, and you should already understand the strategy when it does.)

PLAYING THE MAJORITY PLAY HANDS BEFORE THE FLOP

Now it's time to examine the play of the majority play hands of 6-6, 5-5, 4-4, 3-3, 2-2, A-x suited, and K-Q before the flop, all of them weaker than the "top ten" hands in Chapter 3. Common sense and deception are two important concepts in the play of these hands. I view the pairs 2-2 through 6-6 as basically being of the same value before the flop in limit Hold'em. A-x suited is slightly below the value that I assign these pairs, and K-Q is the weakest.

Calling with Small Pairs

Most theories agree that you should be the first raiser with a pair before the flop, that is, that with your small pair you should usually make it two bets to go. But when it is already two bets to you, a popular theory says you can either call the two bets or fold. Some top pros want you to call two bets with these pairs in order to lure other players into calling and therefore "build the pot" before the flop in the hope that you'll flop a set. So they'll have you passively call someone else's raise before the flop, leaving you hoping that others will call two bets before the flop as well.

Although this sounds good on paper, keep in mind that you'll flop a set roughly once in every eight tries. Now what do you do with your 3-3 when the flop comes down J-10-2? You're forced to fold, because you've let other people into the pot, some of whom probably have you beaten at this point. (If you'd reraised, they would probably have folded.) One advantage "calling to build a pot" does have going for it is that if you miss the flop, you can generally just fold your hand and be done with it. In other words, no thinking is required. If you flop your set, then you jam it, but if you have a bad flop, then you just fold your hand right away. Generally, this is a relatively easy way, and not a bad way, to play limit Hold'em.

Reraising with Small Pairs, Before the Flop

I have a different preference. I like to reraise with a small pair before the flop and then "represent" whatever hits the flop (to your opponents, you *seem* to have started with something before the flop, and to have hit it on the flop). This is a more deceptive approach, allowing a chance to win every pot you play. Imagine having made it three bets with 4-4 over the top of your opponent, and now the flop comes down A-8-2. Your opponent checks to you, and then you bet out with your 4-4, just as if you have A-K. Your opponent now folds his K-Q, and you have won this pot fairly easily.

But let's suppose you play this hand according to the mainstream "calling" theory. You call the two bets with 4-4, and one other player and the big blind also call. The flop comes down A-8-2, and now the big blind checks. Now the original raiser bets out with his K-Q, hoping that no one calls him. By just calling the preflop raise, you've given the K-Q the chance to use deception. The K-Q is now representing an ace! You have to fold your hand right here. You can't call the first bet, because you have to fear that someone has an ace, or maybe the big blind has an eight. You have gone from a position of power to a position of weakness simply by not reraising before the flop—quite a difference.

By reraising, you'll win more pots, but you'll also get yourself into trouble more often. Consider the following scenario. You have three bets in with 4-4, but the original raiser has K-K. He decides just to call your raise and then play his hand hard on the flop if an ace doesn't come. This is a common strategy for people who hold aces or kings. The flop comes down 7d-8d-2c. This appears to be a good flop for you. After all, it's unlikely that the original raiser has a seven or an eight in his hand, so unless you're up against a big pair instead of the more likely two big cards, you're winning at this point. The K-K bets out and you raise him, and now he reraises (three-bets) you.

You have a fair amount of money already invested in this pot. If you had known your opponent had kings, you would have thrown your hand away, but it's also possible that he could have been playing a big flush draw this way. You end up calling him all the way down, only to have him show you K-K. You have just lost a fortune using my reraising approach! Every approach offers its own risks and its own possibilities.

Now let's look at the play of the hand using the mainstream calling approach. You just call two bets with 4-4 before the flop, and now both blinds call. The flop is 7d-8d-2c, and the big blind (who wouldn't have been in the hand using my approach, because the reraise would have pushed him out) bets out, and now the K-K raises to protect what he correctly feels is currently the best hand. You now fold, having lost only three small bets. Clearly, the mainstream approach has done well in this situation.

But if the original raiser had A-K rather than K-K, then my reraising approach would yield better results here. I like my approach because it is mathematically more likely that the first raiser has two big cards than that he has a big pair. But remember, my aggressive approach does lead to more fluctuation in the size of your stack across time, and if you don't have much of a bankroll, pursuing it may put you in an awkward spot.

Now let's look at a few other examples that compare the two approaches to playing small pairs, using my "three bet" theory with the mainstream theory of calling to build a pot.

EXAMPLES

Making It Two Bets with No Callers

You have 4-4 and two people in front of you have folded. According to both theories you make it two bets to go, so that you have a chance to win the blinds before the flop. No need, then, to discuss this case further.

Making It Two Bets with Callers

You have 2-2, and two people have "limped in" (simply called the bet before the flop). My theory says you should raise here. The mainstream theory— "call to build a pot"—can go either way here, but it leans more toward just calling, since two other players have already called ahead of you. The "call" theory is thinking: let's get by for one bet before the flop; then we can fold if we don't flop a set. Not bad thinking, but why not put in one raise and represent something strong with a bet after the flop? For one more bet before the flop and one more after the flop, you may win the whole pot on the flop. And raising does accord nicely with the "building a pot" part of the "calling" theory.

Small Pairs When the Mouse Has Come In Raising

You have 3-3 in late position, and a mouse has raised in front of you (types of players are discussed in Chapter 3, page 42). A mouse raising, as you will recall, is a scary thought indeed! Both theories are now in agreement: the mouse probably has your 3-3 beat with a higher pair. So what to do? My reraising approach doesn't advocate reraising when you're almost certain that you're beat. Folding your hand at this point is clearly the best idea. Why put in your money as a $4\frac{1}{2}$-to-1 underdog to the mouse's higher pair, which he probably has? You can throw away a lot of "majority play hands" and some "top ten hands" when the mouse comes in raising!

But if you feel that others will call the mouse's raise behind you (something possible to probable in a low-stakes game where the other players haven't even noticed that the mouse is someone who doesn't raise very often), then calling is OK. If you do flop a set, then you'll probably win a big pot. Frankly, I would probably call the mouse's raise, thinking that the most I could lose would be two small bets, but the most I could win would be a lot of bets. In this calling scenario, I'm looking to collect from the other players more than from the mouse. In other words, I would be thinking that if I flop a three, I win big; but if I don't, then I'll just fold my hand, having lost little.

Raise and "Isolate" the Jackal
You have 3-3 in the fourth position and a jackal has raised in the second position. My theory says reraise (three-bet) and "isolate" the jackal (play the crazy player one on one) with your 3-3. The "call to build a pot" theory says just call the bet. But even if you subscribe to it, that theory and the notion of isolating the jackal aren't mutually exclusive. Nonetheless, people who like to call and build large pots tend not to use the more aggressive isolation play.

Small Pairs—Don't Call Three Bets!
You have 5-5, and it has been two bet and then three bet in front of you. For the "majority play

hands," as opposed to the "top ten hands," calling three bets is a bad idea. Just fold your 5-5 and live to fight another day. Still, if nearly every hand in your game is being three-bet, then by all means call the three bets! (In a crazy game like that—which by the way, I love to play in—sets tend to play well and win huge pots.) Even at low stakes it is unusual to play in a game where every pot is three-bet, so folding small pairs for three bets is the norm. In general, then, fold all small pairs for three bets unless you know three things: that more or less every hand in your game gets three-bet or four-bet; that your bankroll can handle the wild swings this is almost certainly going to create; and that your emotions can handle things like flopping sets and losing to people who make straights with hands like 2-3 off suit (this can be tough to swallow!).

How to Play A-x Suited Before the Flop

Once you add A-x suited to the arsenal of hands you play, you need to pursue this hand within certain constraints:

1. A-x suited is not a hand you would ever want to call three bets with before the flop. Perhaps if your hand is A-10 or A-J suited, and you're in

the big blind, then it's OK (recall that we covered A-Q and A-K in Chapter 3). But with only a very few exceptions, you don't ever want to call three bets with A-x suited.

2. When no one else has entered the pot in front of you, you should usually make it two bets with this hand. This way your raise seems to be representing a strong hand, and you may just end up winning the blinds if no one calls your raise. With these types of weak hands, picking up the blinds is a good result.

3. When anyone else has already limped into the pot in front of you (just called one bet), you should call that one bet. For the intermediate-level player, this play is slightly better than making it two bets. If you then hit the flop, you can play your hand hard, but if you miss the flop, you can fold your hand, having lost only one bet.

4. If someone raises in front of you, then just call the two bets. The one exception is that you could three-bet a jackal with A-10 or A-J suited.

I don't think giving you any more examples of what to do before the flop with A-x suited would help very much at this point. You now have the basic principles. (I hope, by the way, that I'm not driving you crazy with all these rules followed so closely by all these exceptions! That's just the way poker is. Personality and relative hand strength are always factors.)

Playing K-Q Before the Flop

I think we can safely move on now to the play of K-Q before the flop. When you're considering calling a raise with K-Q, pause and consider some more, because most of the time your hand is beaten! In fact, if a mouse were to raise, I would just throw this hand away before the flop. A certain small percentage of the time, the first raiser will have A-K or A-Q, in which case you're in particularly bad shape! Let's look at a quick list of rules for K-Q:

1. Never call three bets with K-Q. You just don't want to get yourself in too deep with this hand before the flop. If it's three bets to you to go, then you can be almost certain that your hand is beaten, and probably in bad shape.
2. Always raise it to two bets with K-Q before the flop. Whether someone else has limped in in front of you or not, make it two bets to go. Representing hands in Hold'em is a strong way to play poker.

3. If it's two bets to go to you, then use your best judgment regarding whether you should call the two bets, raise it to three bets, or fold. If a mouse made it two bets, then fold your hand; if anyone else made it two bets, then call; if a jackal made it two bets, then sometimes you might make it three bets to go (this is more of an advanced play). But what if an elephant made it two bets to go and then a mouse called the two bets? Here, too, use your best judgment. Calling and folding are both OK, but when you're on the fence, don't forget to take position into account (it's a much easier call on or near the button).

The play of K-Q before the flop is thus relatively simple. Notice that it is almost exactly like playing A-x suited before the flop. The only difference is that with A-x suited you should call just one bet when there are limpers before the flop, whereas with K-Q you should make it two bets with other limpers. (When you have A-x suited you're hoping for more opponents.)

Playing before the flop is the easiest part of the "majority play hands" approach. Now it's time to move on to the most difficult part of playing these hands: how to play on the flop.

PLAYING THE MAJORITY PLAY
HANDS ON THE FLOP

Although you can still use "raise to find out where you are" as a strategy with "majority play" hands, it's not as powerful a move as it was in playing the top ten hands. Now that we're playing the majority play hands as well, two things will change dramatically. The first is your table image; the second is the power of the hands you're playing.

Your *table image* is the way the other players in the game are likely to be viewing you. When you're playing the top ten hands only, people will fear your hands when you raise the pots, because you're playing only very powerful hands—if they've been paying attention (but remember, some people won't pay attention, no matter how consistently you play). Now that you're playing some weaker hands too, your opponents will fear your raises less and therefore call (or raise) you more.

When you add the "majority play hands" to your acceptable starting-hand list, you'll find yourself playing well over twice as many hands as before. Therefore the power of the average hand that you're playing will go way down, and in time your more astute opponents will begin to perceive that as well (your table image is now altered). Both of these changes will have a direct impact on the way you should play your hands on the flop. You should continue to raise to find out where you are in some hands, but now discretion and deception become very important.

Shakespeare, as we know, wrote that discretion is the better part of valor. In poker, valor (courage) and aggressiveness are winning traits. You will win many more pots by playing your hands aggressively, but it takes a lot of valor to raise someone on a flop of Q-J-2 when you're holding pocket tens! Shakespeare never played poker, but in Hold'em there are indeed times when discretion is the better part of valor. There is a time to throw your hand away after the flop, rather than putting up a fight. Sometimes, "saving bets" is the name of the game in Hold'em; and the only way you can save them is by folding your hand in a timely manner.

For example, if you three-bet with 4-4 and three opponents take a flop, and then the flop comes down Q-9-2, you're better off not calling any bets or making any raises. Folding is a pretty good choice at this point. Even if somehow your 4-4 was the best hand preflop, when you're facing three opponents who have hung in to play for three bets, and you see two high cards on the flop, there's a pretty good chance that your little pair is now losing. Yes, you could be up against A-K, 7-6 suited, and J-10 suited, which would technically mean you're still winning. Notice, though, that even if that rather unlikely "best-case scenario" was in fact what you had wandered into, you will lose if any ace, king, jack, ten, eight, or six hits on the turn or the river. Save your valor for another hand.

EXAMPLES

To give you a greater sense of what you need to do on the flop while playing the "majority play hands," I'll lead you through several examples.

Playing Small Pairs (2-2 Through 6-6) on the Flop: Pump It or Dump It

In general, if there are four people in the pot when the flop comes down and you have a small pair, you need to flop a set in order to continue playing your hand. Of course, if you have 6-6, and the flop comes down 3-4-5, this too is a good flop, although certainly not as strong as flopping the set. When you have this kind of flop, you want to raise to protect your hand, because although there's a reasonable chance that you have the best hand at the moment, all you have at this point is a pair of sixes, a hand clearly vulnerable to overcards that could give someone else a higher pair. Of course, if you get callers and then make your straight (preferably with the deuce, because then you'll get a lot of action from anyone holding an ace), you'll want to continue raising—for the same reason you want to raise when you flop a set: you have the best hand and want to "pump it."

When the flop comes down J-Q-2 to your 6-6 with four players in the pot, then use some discretion and (in most cases) fold your hand: "dump it." The "pump it" tactic is used either to protect your hand, by raising to eliminate your opponents on the flop, or to get more money into the pot when you have a strong flop. "Dump it" is used to save bets, by using your best discretion to fold your hand on the flop, thus losing no more bets.

Playing Small Pairs on the Flop

You have 4-4 in the fourth position, and the player in the second position (two seats to the left of the big blind) makes it two bets to go. You're playing my theory—"three-bet with small pairs"—before the flop, so you make it three bets. No one else calls, and the flop is Q-10-3. The player in the second position then bets out into you and you raise him, thus "representing" a queen (or perhaps K-K or A-A) but also gaining information. If your opponent reraises you, then either you're already beaten (this is more likely) or your opponent has a straight draw, and it's time for a decision. If you feel you have him beat at this point, then you may want to reraise him. Or you might decide that your opponent has you beaten and fold your hand on the flop. You might decide simply to call his reraise on the flop and defer a decision to call or fold when you see what drops on fourth street. I would call one more bet and make a decision on fourth street heavily weighted toward folding, but trust your instincts here.

If your opponent just calls your raise, then he may still have you beaten, with something like A-10 or Q-J. But if he doesn't have you beaten, then he most likely has some sort of straight draw like K-J, A-J, or A-K. Therefore, any nine, jack, king, or ace would be a terrible card for you on fourth street.

Let's look at the way this hand would be played on the flop if you had just called the two bets with your 4-4 before the flop. In this case, it's likely that at least one other player will have called the two bets before the flop. Suppose one of them was the big blind, since it costs him only one more bet. Now the big blind checks after the Q-10-3 flop, and the preflop raiser bets out. You have to use a bit more discretion here because you also have to worry about the big blind behind you. I would probably just call the bet in this case and see what the big blind does. If the big blind were to fold, then I would make a decision about this hand later, on fourth street. (In this case, it's all about how you read your opponent on fourth street.) But if the big blind were to raise the bet on the flop, then I would just fold my hand right there. And if the big blind were to call the bet, then I would assume that he has some sort of straight draw, or maybe a mediocre piece of the flop with something like 10-8 or A-3.

Suppose now that the button player and the big blind both call the two bets before the flop. So we have the second position making it two bets, you calling the two bets with 4-4 in the fourth position, and now the button and the big blind calling the two bets as well. The flop comes down Q-10-3. Now the big blind checks and the original raiser bets out on the flop. What do you do? With three other opponents still in this hand and two overcards on the board (Q-10), folding is the proper play. Moreover, considering that the second-position original raiser has bet out into you, and that there are two other people behind you yet to act, this scenario is a bit scary. You just have to give up and fold.

Playing Small Pairs: Flopping a Set

You have 2-2 on the button, the second position raises, and then the fourth position calls the two bets. You play in my style and make it three bets to go, everyone calls, and the flop comes down 2-4-J. You have flopped a set! You should put in as many raises as you can, both to build the pot and to protect your hand.

If you've used the other approach and just called before the flop with your 2-2, and then get your 2-4-J flop, nothing changes in your postflop approach. You still put in as many bets and raises as you can in order to build a pot and protect your hand. No matter how you play your small pair before the flop, when you hit a set it's time to "ram and jam" (raise and reraise). Sets usually win or lose (a majority of the time sets win) pretty-good-size pots.

Playing Small Pairs: Good Flops, Protecting Your Hand

Assume that you have 6-6 in the small blind, the third position has raised before the flop, the fifth position has called the raise, and now the flop comes down 2-4-5.

Now it's your turn to act. You bet out, and the third position calls the bet. Now the fifth position makes it two bets, so you reraise (making it three bets) in order to protect your hand. This is a great flop for your hand, and you need to reraise in order to get rid of the original raiser. At this point, the only hands that can beat you are overpairs, and in any case, you have a straight draw to go with your hand. Maybe the original raiser has K-Q and your reraise forces him to fold his hand. If you don't drive him out, you may lose the pot to him by allowing him to call just one more bet in the hope of catching a king or a queen.

Suppose you're taking the approach where you just call the two bets before the flop, and the big blind calls. Now it's your turn to act. Because you haven't shown too much strength before the flop, you might want to try checking with your now powerful hand, and then raising when someone else bets out into you. Sometimes the "check-raise" plays can help you eliminate your opponents and therefore help you protect your hand. But betting out into the flop works well also. In either case, you want to "ram and jam" (raise and reraise) your hand with this flop in order to protect it.

Playing Small Pairs: Terrible Flops
Some flops are so bad for small pairs that you should just run for cover, no matter whether

you've just called two bets before the flop or made it three bets. If the flop comes down Q-K-A, it's time to fold as soon as possible! Of course, if I had been using my three-bet approach I would bet on the flop when it was my turn, on the off chance that all my opponents might fold their hands, giving me the pot right there. It could also happen that I get called on the flop and then hit my set card on either fourth street or the river. Such things are possible. But I would not call a bet on this flop; I would not call a bet on the turn; I would not call a bet on the river; I would not bet on either fourth street or the river. All I would do in this case is make that one bet on the flop when it's my turn to bet.

Playing Small Pairs: Good Flops

When you have 4-4 in a pot, flops like J-J-3 or 10-10-2 or 9-9-3 are good for your hand; there is in fact an excellent chance that your two pair is the best hand at the table at this point. So put in some bets and raises, for two reasons: first, to find out if you do have the best hand; second, to protect your hand. When you face mixed overcards like J-10-3, you're in trouble, but when a big pair lands on the flop, it's much less likely that someone already holds the key card. For example, in the J-J-3 flop, there are only two jacks left in the deck; had the flop come J-10-3, there are six cards—three jacks and three tens—in the deck that would beat you. So with the J-J-3 flop, your pocket fours are the best hand unless someone has a higher pair or one of the two remaining jacks (both are unlikely).

Reraising Before the Flop Leads to Betting on the Flop

When you're playing the small pairs the way I suggest (reraising with them before the flop), a lot of times you'll end up playing three-bet pots against only one or two opponents. When this happens, be sure you bet the flop aggressively, so as to gain information about what your opponents may have. Suppose for example that you've made it three bets before the flop with 3-3, and then the flop comes down A-K-9. If your lone remaining opponent checks, then go ahead and bet once. You never know—he may just fold for the one bet. Perhaps he too has a small pair, or he holds 10-8 suited or something of that sort.

Playing A-x Suited on the Flop: Hit It or Fold It

In the discussion of preflop situations, I said that if no one else has raised the pot before the flop, and you have A-x suited, then you should make it two bets to go. In general, if you've done that but missed the flop, you should bet out once anyway, thus representing that you've hit it. If an opponent calls your bet on the flop when you've missed the flop, prepare to fold your hand soon. There is no need to get too involved with A-x suited if you miss the flop, and no warrant for bluffing off too much money with this hand. If you're the raiser before the flop, then take one "shot" (bluff) at the pot and give up if you get called.

Where someone else *has* raised the pot before the flop, I've been recommending that you just call his two bets. In general, if you've done that but then missed the flop, then you should fold your hand. Again, there's no need for you to get involved in such a pot by calling or raising. Just throw your hand away, save some chips, and forget about it.

With A-x suited you'll see a lot of different flops that hit part or all of your hand. You may have Ad-7d when the flop comes down J-10-7; this one is trouble for you (because you hit just enough of the flop that you may decide to play on until the end and lose a bunch of chips). You may have Ad-7d when the flop comes down A-7-4, a terrific flop for you. You may have Ad-7d when the flop comes down 8-7-2, a reasonably good flop for you. You may have Ad-7d when the flop comes down 7-5-2, a strong flop for you (top pair with top kicker). Finally, there are dream flops for Ad-7d like Kd-Jd-2d (ace-high flush) and A-A-7 (top full house).

So there are a lot of ways to hit A-x suited, some of them good and others bad. The interesting thing is that you may win your biggest pot with the 7-5-2 flop! Why? On those two "dream flops" I just mentioned, how much action can you expect to get from other players? You already have most of the cards that would get someone interested in playing. But on the 7-5-2 flop, people may sense a bluff and try what they think is a *resteal* (they raise on a bluff because they believe you're trying to steal the pot). In poker, you never know which hands or flops will win you the biggest pot of the night. Just be prepared to play your hand as well as you can.

I'll never forget a pot I once played holding A-7 at the World Series of Poker. The year was 1994, and we were down to about 40 players left in a no-limit Hold'em event. First place was $220,000, and as with any WSOP event, both money and history were at stake.

Two players to my right was a jackal from Europe who was reraising everyone while holding any kind of hand. He was a real nuisance to me, because he kept reraising me and stealing all the pots that he and I were going after. In fact, he was reraising everyone at the table and outplaying us all after the flop with his big bluffs. He had played this very dangerous style to near perfection, parlaying his chips to over $65,000. I also had about $65,000 in front of me, which is a ton of chips. This jackal and I were the chip leaders at a time when the average chip stack in the tournament was less than $15,000. Conventional wisdom at this point would suggest that neither one of us should play a big pot against the other. Why risk a boatload of chips in a single hand, when we could both just coast in to the final table with our huge stacks of chips? A cardinal sin at this point would be to get involved in a big pot with each of us holding really weak hands.

So much for conventional wisdom and cardinal sins! I soon found myself raising it to $2,000 to go before the flop with my A-7. The jackal was sitting in the big blind this hand, and he decided to reraise me by making it $8,000 to go. Perhaps he smelled my weakness and was just trying to force me out of the pot with his weak hand. He was right—I was weak—but he didn't count on the fact that I had smelled the weakness in his reraise. So I reraised it again to $20,000 to go before the flop. Again, I think the jackal smelled some weakness in me, and in any case he decided to call my $20,000 bet. Now the flop came down 7c-5d-4d, and he bet out $15,000. I decided that top pair was enough to allow me to move all-in against him because I thought I had the best hand. Frankly, I wasn't hoping for a call. So I moved all-in for $45,000. (I raised him $30,000!)

The jackal then called me quickly, and the next two cards to hit the board were the two worst cards I could think of! First the 6c came off the deck and then the Qd (7c-5d-4d-6c-Qd), so that the flush draw and a straight draw had both hit the board! I stared in disbelief at the board. What had I done? I had just put in $65,000 with an incredibly weak hand! I could have waited patiently for some strong hands and made the final table fairly easily. I couldn't beat anything anymore. The flush draw beat me, some straight draws beat me, a set beat me, and an overpair beat me! But he was the first guy to flip his hand faceup, and he was taking a long time to do it.

I was thinking, "Just show me your hand, and I'll leave this tournament feeling sick about my awful play." With $130,000 in the pot in a tournament where no one else had even $30,000, the winner of this one pot would have an excellent chance of winning the tournament. Finally, he flipped up his hand and said, "One pair." I stared in amazement at his hand: 7-9 off suit, which gave him a pair of sevens with a nine kicker! I had a pair of sevens with an ace kicker, and the pot was mine! My good read of this jackal paid off, and from there I cruised easily down to the final three players. My attitude quickly changed from "Phil, you idiot, how did you let yourself get $65,000 into this pot with this hand?" to "Phil, baby, great play, great read, well done!" Eventually, I finished in second place and collected $110,000. Here was a story illustrating how an A-7 can pay off big when you merely hit a good flop with it. But please don't try this at home.

EXAMPLES

Now it's time to move on and give you some examples of how you should play A-x suited on the flop. In general, with A-x suited, we "hit it or fold it."

Playing A-x Suited on the Flop: Flush Draw

Suppose that an elephant has made it two bets in the second position before the flop and then a jackal in the fourth position has called the two bets. Now you call on the button with Ah-3h, and the big blind calls as well. The flop is 9h-Qh-2s, and the big blind checks. The elephant bets and the jackal raises. What do you do? You have flopped the "nut" (best) flush draw. If another heart comes off the deck, then you have made an ace-high flush.

This is a reasonably strong flop for your hand. With this strong draw, you'll make the flush about one-third of the time, and occasionally you may win simply by hitting your ace, so you must either call the two bets or raise it to three bets to go. My instinct in this case would be to raise. Who knows what the jackal has in this hand? He may have a flush draw or a straight draw, in which case you have him beat with your ace high at this point. Your raise may eliminate the elephant (who may have the best hand!) and get you one on one with the jackal, whom you may have beaten. The worst-case scenario for you, if you make it three bets to go, is that the elephant makes it four bets to go and you end up having to call one more bet.

In general, I recommend playing a nut-flush draw very aggressively on the flop, especially when you have position, as you do in this example. This hand all but requires that you call a bet with it on fourth street, and if it were mine I would want to put in a lot of bets on the flop and then bluff at the pot on fourth street even if a bad card comes off. Alternatively, I'd put in a lot of bets on the flop and call down one opponent on the end with my measly ace high if there's any chance that this opponent was drawing to something as well. Sometimes the size of the pot that you create by playing the nut-flush draw aggressively will necessitate your calling on the river with merely ace high, because the size of the pot may tempt other players who are on inferior draws to make desperation bluffs at you. You win these often enough, with your ace-high river call, to justify this play.

Playing A-x Suited: Bad Flop

Suppose that a jackal has raised before the flop, and you have called his raise with Ad-5d, and then the big blind calls as well. If the flop comes down Js-Qh-3d and the big blind checks and the jackal bets, fold your hand. You have missed the flop (you don't have either a pair, a straight draw, or a flush draw); you have only two bets in the pot at this point; and you were the caller before the flop, not the raiser. There is no warrant for getting further involved in this hand.

Suppose now that a jackal has called one bet before the flop, and you've raised it with your Ad-5d. Then the big blind and the jackal both call and the flop comes down Js-Qh-3d. If they both check to you on the flop, then go ahead and bet once on the flop. They may both fold at this point. If one of them does bet into you, just fold your hand. Other than taking one shot at the pot on the flop when you were the preflop raiser with A-x suited, what you really want to do when you miss the flop is fold your hand.

Playing A-x Suited: Hitting Second Pair

A jackal in the second position raises before the flop, and you call with As-9s in fifth position. The button and the big blind call as well. The flop is 10h-9h-2s, and the jackal bets out into you. This situation seems to be a good time for a raise. To have you beaten right now, someone has to have a ten in his hand or an overpair (a set or two pair are also possible). You also know that the jackal could have anything at this point in the hand.

Let's try the same situation, but let's say that the big blind bets out this time and then the jackal raises on the flop. What do you do? It's time to use that newly developed reading power you've been working on. There are two possibilities here: you have the best hand or not. With this flop (10h-9h-2s), it's possible that you still have the best hand with your As-9s. Perhaps one of your opponents has J-9, and the other has the J-Q for an open-ended straight draw. Maybe one of your opponents has a straight draw and the other has a flush draw. But you may also be in a lot of trouble with the way that the action came down on this flop. Perhaps one of your opponents has a ten (for a pair of tens) and the other has a flush draw. If this is the case, then you need to hit one of two aces left in the deck (the Ah makes a flush), one of two nines left, or consecutive spades (called "runner-runner," not something you want to depend on!) for a backdoor flush. So if one of your opponents has you beaten, then you're really an underdog to win this pot. Whether you call two bets or fold in this case depends on how you read your opponents.

Playing A-x Suited: OK Flop

Suppose you've called an elephant's early-position raise with Ac-6c on the button. The big blind calls the raise as well, and the flop comes down Jh-Jd-6h. Now the big blind bets out and the jackal raises. What do you do? Read, read, and read your opponents. If it were my hand and if I didn't have a read on my opponents, I would reraise (make it three bets) to find out where I am, especially given that the raiser was a jackal. Your opponents need to have an overpair or three jacks to have your two pair beaten at this point in the hand. They may have the three jacks, or they may have 6-7 or K-6 or a smaller pair or a flush draw. Raise it in this spot, unless you have a strong feeling that you're beaten, in which case fold.

Playing A-x Suited: Marginal Flop

Suppose you've called an elephant's early-position raise with As-10s and then three other players call, including the big blind. The flop comes down Jd-10h-8c, and the big blind bets out and the elephant calls. What do you think, and what do you do? I wouldn't raise, because I figure that there is an excellent chance that the big blind has me beaten, and with five players in the pot, what are the chances that I have the best hand? But calling and folding are reasonable options. I would lean toward calling, but with two other people behind you and the big blind leading out, I could also make a pretty reasonable case for folding your hand right there. What did the elephant, the original raiser, call the one bet with on this flop? It seems pretty likely that he has A-Q, A-K, or K-Q, all of which would give him a straight draw. The reasons why I lean toward calling a bet on the flop in this situation are these:

1. You may have the best hand.
2. There are already six big bets in this pot.

3. Calling will cost only one more small bet, and perhaps both opponents behind you will fold their hands.

4. You may hit an ace or a ten on fourth street and wind up winning this pot because you called that one bet on the flop.

5. It's possible that everyone will check the rest of the way (no one will bet on fourth street or the river) and that you win the pot because you called one small bet on the flop. (Don't hold your breath hoping for this to happen!)

Playing A-x Suited: Flopping a Draw

Suppose that a mouse in second position has raised it up before the flop and the jackal on the button has called. You then called as well in the big blind with Ad-8d, and the flop is 5d-6c-7s. Generally, when you flop an open-ended straight draw (you need a four or a nine to make your hand) in Hold'em, especially when you're drawing to the big side (in this case a nine-high straight as opposed to having A-4 and drawing to the small side or eight-high straight), you're well advised to play this hand all the way to try and hit it. What do you do now?

You know that you are going to have to call on

the flop, and on the turn as well, if you miss making the hand on fourth street. You also know that the mouse has a strong hand and that the jackal could have anything. I would be thinking, "I hope the mouse has A-K so that I can bluff him out of this pot." (We all know how tightly the mouse plays!) I would also be hoping that the jackal has a hand that I can beat, but that he can bet with, for example A-4 or K-8 or J-8 or some other straight draw. Perhaps I would check with my hand, hoping that the mouse checks and the jackal bets. Then I could check-raise, making it two bets to the mouse and therefore forcing him to fold his A-K or A-Q. Of course, what I really want to do is complete my straight on the turn or the river.

You could also decide to bet right out into the mouse on the flop, to see what he does. The mouse would either call you or raise you; it's hard to imagine him folding this flop, just because he's a mouse, which means he had a pretty strong hand before the flop. If he were to call me, I would try to bluff him out on the next two rounds of betting, thinking he couldn't call me down with A-K—because he's a mouse! If he were to raise me on the flop, then I would call him and check to him on the next two rounds of betting (unless I were to make my straight). I'm assuming that the mouse would just call on the flop with A-K and raise me with any overpair.

Playing A-x Suited: Second Pair with Mouse

Suppose that a mouse has raised in the third position and an elephant has called on the button, before the flop. You call with As-8s in the big blind because it's only one more bet to you in the big blind. Normally you wouldn't call the mouse's raise with this hand, but you're getting a discount! The flop comes down 9-8-3. What do you do here? I'd want to bet out here to see what the mouse does. If the mouse were to raise me, then I'd probably call the bet, but I'd fold my hand if the mouse bet on fourth street (unless I'd caught an ace or an eight). If the mouse just called me on the flop, then I'd figure that I have him beat (I'd put the mouse on A-K or A-Q) and I'd continue to bet with my hand all the way.

If the elephant were to put in a raise on the flop, then you'd have to read him the best that you could. You'd want to call his raise on the flop and see what card comes up on fourth street and whether the elephant bets on fourth street or not.

Playing A-x Suited: Strong Flops, Slow-Play

When you hit a really strong flop for your A-x suited

hand, you have to decide how to collect the maximum number of bets. Usually, you can win the maximum by jamming the pot (putting in as many bets and raises as you can) after the flop. But sometimes, in order to give the impression that you're weak, you need to slow-play your hand—put no bets or raises in on the flop. If you've just flopped a "monster" (a huge hand) and someone bets out into you on the flop, you might want to just call one bet in order to draw your other opponents into the pot. Why raise everyone out of the pot when you flop a big hand? If your table image is weak or wild, you can raise on the flop because no one thinks you have anything anyway. If your table image is strong or tight, you're better off letting someone else bet your hand for you, even at the cost of missing some bets on the flop, in order to increase the chance that you can collect lots of bets on the last two rounds, when the limits are doubled. Let's look at some more examples.

Playing A-x Suited: Strong Flop, Slow-Play or Not

Suppose that a jackal in the first position raises and you call with Ac-4c in the third position (even in this early position, this is a pretty easy call against a jackal). Now the fifth position and both blinds call the raise as well. The flop comes down 10c-9c-6c, and now the big blind bets out and the jackal raises. What do you do now? You have flopped the nut flush! The others can't beat you unless they flopped a set and the board gives them a pair, or unless they catch perfectly on both of the next two streets (you can't live in fear of runner-runner).

If you reraise and make it three bets to go on the flop, you might drive out the fifth-position player and both blinds, and that's not what you want. You're not going to drive out anyone who flopped a set (that is, anyone who has a reasonable chance to beat you); you're going to drive out only people who need a miracle to beat you. This is the time when you should just call the two bets and hope that everyone else calls as well. Or better yet, just call, hoping that everyone else calls, and hope that the big blind reraises it. This is a time to keep as many players in the pot as you can on the flop, because in the next two rounds of betting the limits are doubled.

If everyone checks to you on the flop, then you should bet out one bet rather than checking. After all, you have to give the other players a chance to check-raise you on the flop! You have to start building a pot sometime, and the flop is the place to make sure that you get at least one bet in the pot.

Making the pot larger now may encourage people whose hands are still trailing badly to call for the size of the pot later (they may call bets later because they want to try to win the big pot out there), when they (although they won't know it) have little or no chance to win.

Trying to lure in the maximum number of bets in a hand is a nice problem to have, but doing it well every time can be tricky. Most of the time, in most pots, no one gets the maximum anyway when playing with a monster hand. After all, we can't see everyone else's hole cards. So just strive to get as close to the maximum as you can.

Playing A-x Suited: Strong Flops, Slow-Play?

When you have Ad-7d, and the flop is Ah-7h-3s, you want opponents in the pot, but you want to make sure that you protect your hand as well. In other circles, this would be known as wanting to eat your cake and have it too. Suppose that four people are in the pot, and the player in front of you bets out. What do you do? You could just call and let people in for one bet, but you might then let 8s-8h in the pot for one bet and then lose the pot to the 8s-8h when an eight comes off (in this case you'd lose a lot of chips as well!) or lose it to a heart-heart finish. I would raise on the flop to protect my hand and build that big pot right there and then. Maybe your surviving opponent has As-Ks, and maybe he'll reraise you on the flop.

When you flop the nut flush or a full house with your A-x suited, it's time to try to extract from your opponents all the bets you can. This may well include slow-playing your hand on the flop. When you flop two pair with your A-x suited, then it's time to protect your hand by jamming the flop as much as possible. You've flopped a strong hand, but it's still much too vulnerable for slow-playing. If you flop trips (three of a kind) when it comes 7-7-J and you have A-7, then it's time to examine the situation more closely. Should you slow-play or not? How many opponents are there in the hand? Are there two to a suit on the board on the flop? Generally, I will jam it with my trips in order to protect my hand. Most people slow-play too much, and they risk letting opponents back into positions where they can beat the slow-player. Not only is this a big financial setback; it's the kind of defeat that can put a player on tilt. (You will hear the word "tilt" every time you play poker in a casino. It is a very common poker word that means being too troubled to play your usual game.)

We could talk all day about how to play your A-x suited after a marginal flop. What it really comes down to, though, is this: when you have a marginal flop with A-x suited, try to read your opponents to decide what to do with your hand. If you feel that they are weak, raise. If you feel that they are strong, fold. Don't forget to raise to find out where you are at if you aren't quite sure. This play is a great way to sort things out in your mind.

Playing K-Q on the Flop: Hit It or Fold It

I consider K-Q the weakest of my "majority play hands." Some pros may consider A-6 suited the weakest, because one might make a straight with A-2 suited. Others may consider 2-2 the weakest. A good argument can be made for any of these hands being the weakest of the majority play hands. Be that as it may, K-Q gets my vote for the weakest hand of the lot. This is a hand you need to hit on the flop if you are going to continue playing it.

Of course, when the flop is 4-10-J, and you hold K-Q, then you have an open-ended straight draw. In this case, you need to play the hand all the way to the end, in the hope of hitting your straight. The trouble flops for K-Q are something like A-Q-2 or A-K-5. You have flopped second pair (the kings or queens) with top kicker, and this hand is just strong enough to get you into trouble. You can't beat any ace, but you can beat almost every other hand. Of course, it's always nice to see K-Q-4 (top two pair) or 10-J-A (nut straight) when you have K-Q! (Andy Glazer once elbowed me in the side and told me that the first time he ever played no-limit in a live game, he had K-Q and the flop came K-Q-4. His opponent had been holding pocket fours, and you can probably envision the ensuing carnage. Notwithstanding Andy's traumatic introduction to no-limit, if you flop top two pair in limit poker, you should push pretty hard.)

When you do hit K-Q, it is important to protect your hand by jamming the flop. K-9-2 and K-J-4 are pretty strong flops when you have K-Q. Without going into any further examples, suffice to say that K-Q is the kind of hand that you fold if you miss the flop, but jam with if you hit the flop, period.

HOW TO PLAY THE MAJORITY PLAY HANDS ON FOURTH STREET

If you have made it to fourth street with any of these hands, then presumably you've hit something on the flop. Fourth street is the time to dump those hands that you decided were no good on the flop, now that the bets have doubled in size. This discussion will be rather short, since judgment is now the key to whether or not you continue to bet, call, or raise with your hand. Obviously, if you've hit a strong hand or a good drawing hand on the flop, then you'll continue to play the hand in some manner. If you flopped a set, two pair, a straight, or a flush, then you'll be doing a lot of betting and raising (jamming the pot) on fourth street. If you have flopped a strong draw, then you'll either be in the lead in the betting or just calling other people's bets at this point in the hand, depending on how you played your draw on the flop.

Fourth street is also the time to evaluate whether or not your opponent has hit his draw. Sometimes it's obvious that he's hit his hand; he'll reveal that by being easy to read. Perhaps he'll all but jump out of his seat when the card comes off the deck! At other times, the card that comes off the deck is the one you knew would be the worst possible card for you, and now you're almost certain you're beaten.

Sometimes, of course, you're the one who hits the draw on fourth street, and now you have to decide how to win the most from your hand, from here on out. Of course, this is a nice problem to have! Maybe you need to jam the pot, or perhaps you need to "smooth-call" someone else's bet—merely call when you have a raising hand—in order to lure other players into the pot at this point.

EXAMPLES

The following are examples of smooth-calling, jamming the pot, raising to protect your hand, and folding.

Smooth-Calling

When you have A-x suited and you hit your nut flush draw on fourth street, you may want to smooth-call someone else's bet in order to win the maximum with your hand. Let's say there are four opponents in the hand against you. The first opponent bets out into you, and you decide to raise him in order to build the pot. Now the next two opponents fold, and the original bettor looks you in the eye and says, "I know you wouldn't raise me here unless you had a flush, so I fold." How much money have you made after hitting your nut flush? One big bet! Why did you raise out the two opponents behind you?

If you were the last person to act and someone bet out into you, then I can understand the raise, because you would already have several people in for one bet, and people who have called one bet rarely drop out for one more. Now suppose that instead of raising, you smooth-call your opponents' bets. Now one of the two other opponents behind you calls the bet as well. On the end, the first opponent bets into you again, but this time you raise (smooth-calling the river bet is rarely if ever a good move), and you get called by both of your remaining two opponents. How many bets have you won this time? Six big bets! All because you smooth-called the bet on fourth street, and, presumably, allowed your opponents to hit good cards for their hands on the last card. (Of course, it's actually a bad card for them, because it didn't improve them enough to win, only enough to lose more money!)

In 2001, in the $7,500 buy-in no-limit Hold'em championship event at the U.S. Poker Championships at the Taj Mahal in Atlantic City, a smooth-call worked for me to perfection. I called a $200 bet with A-A in the first position before the flop. Now Men "The Master" Nguyen, in the small blind, called with 5-6 off suit, and the big blind checked. The flop was A-7-3, and we all checked again; this was the second time this hand that I checked with the best possible hand in order to "trap" my opponents. The next card was a seven for A-7-3-7, and I had made top full house (aces full of sevens).

My opponents both checked to me again, and

now I bet out $200 into the $600 pot. Men called the $200, trying to hit a four for a straight, which would have cost him thousands of dollars more if he had hit it, since I already had a full house. The big blind now raised me $500 (this hand was developing beautifully for me). I decided that I needed to reraise right here in order to give the big blind the chance to give me all his chips (in case he had a seven in his hand), but I didn't want to reraise too much and lose him either. So I reraised $1,000 more, Men folded, and the big blind called me.

On the end, a harmless card came off the deck and my remaining opponent checked to me. I went ahead and bet $2,000, hoping for a call, and my opponent called me very quickly. So I won the hand, and it's very unlikely that I could have extracted another $3,000 from this opponent if I had bet aggressively from the beginning. In fact, if I had raised before the flop in this hand, all my opponents would have folded their hands then and there.

Deceptive plays like smooth-calling and slow-playing generally offer bigger payoffs in pot-limit or no-limit than they do in limit, where you can't grab one giant bet from someone on the end; but even in limit these plays are an important part of the good player's arsenal.

Jamming the Pot

This is the counterpart of the example of slow-playing given above. Sometimes, when you hold the nut hand, you just need to jam the pot on fourth street, in order to make the pot as big as it possibly can be. But it's hard to know the right time to jam the pot, rather than smooth-calling someone else's bet. Generally, it depends on whether someone has bet right in front of you or not. If someone has, then you usually want to smooth-call the bet. But if someone has bet and several others have already called that bet, then it's time to go ahead and raise it up.

Protecting Your Hand with a Raise

The principle of protecting your hand by way of a raise is also very important in Hold'em. ("Protecting your hand" is all about making raises when you have a strong hand, so that you can eliminate players, thus giving yourself a better chance to win that hand.) It can mean the difference between winning and losing a pot. Suppose that you have Ac-3c (A-x suited), and garner two pair with Ad-10d-3s on the flop. Now on fourth street 9c comes off the deck for Ad-10d-3s-9c. Someone now bets into you, and you just call the bet. But because you just called the bet, you let a jackal in with K-Q, and he hits a jack on the end to make a straight. Clearly, even the jackal would have folded his "belly buster" (inside straight draw) for two big bets; but for just one, he was able to dream about a jack and convince himself that hitting a king or queen might win also. Because you didn't protect your hand here by raising, you wound up paying the ultimate price in poker; you lost a pot that you should have won.

Folding Your Hand

When you're involved in a big multiway pot and there's been a lot of raising on the flop, watch out for indications that the drawing hands have hit on fourth street. Suppose you have 6-6 and the flop comes down 2d-3s-4d. On the flop you have three opponents all putting in some bets. Still, you're pretty sure that your hand is the best hand on the flop. But what if the worst possible card for you comes off on fourth street? Then what do you do? To me the worst possible card here is Ad. If Ad comes off the deck, then the straight draw (any five in your opponent's hand), the flush draw (two diamonds in an opponent's hand), and any ace (like A-K or A-4) all get there and beat you. If this card comes off of the deck, then you'd better look to exit stage left immediately.

When you face a situation like this, ask yourself, "What are they holding that's driving them to put all this money into the pot on the flop?" Probably straight draws, flush draws, pairs, and ace high. Folding your hand on fourth street wisely when the draws appear to have been hit is considered an art form.

PLAYING THE MARGINAL PLAY HANDS ON THE RIVER

In the discussion of beginners' strategy for the top ten hands on the river (Chapter 3), I advocated making a lot of calls on the river, because of the large size of the pots with the top ten hands. In other words, the "pot odds" are there for you to call on the end with a top ten hand. This thinking is still somewhat applicable here, but now we're dealing with some weaker hands. Often, in my advice to beginners, my examples would have you in the lead with a strong hand (you're the bettor), and it would be your opponents who were calling *you* down. Now, with the weaker marginal-play hands, you will often be calling your opponents' bets.

Sometimes, situations will come up where you're calling someone down with your A-3 (calling all the way to the end) and a board of As-Ks-4h-7c, and then the last card is Js and someone else bets into you as well. In this case you were calling just one opponent, whose hand probably had your pair of aces with a weak kicker beaten. Now, when a third party bets out into both of you when the flush card hits, folding your hand would seem to be the wise move.

But you may also end up with A-10 and a board of 10s-Js-4d-5h, and then see the river produce Qh. Now what do you do? If there had been a lot of action on the flop here, then you were probably playing against either a spade flush draw, a straight draw, a pair of jacks, or an overpair. With Qh on the river, you can now beat only the flush draw, assuming that the flush draw didn't have a queen with it. The point is that you may have already been in trouble with the A-10, but with this last card and two other opponents still in the action, you shouldn't even think about calling on the river. Again, playing the marginal-play hands, as opposed to the top ten hands, may put you into some bad situations when it's time to ponder calling on the river.

You're still getting pot odds to call someone on the river—the payoff could be huge—but if you can make four or five prudent and well-timed folds a night, that will add up to some serious money by the end of the year! Learning when to call with your marginal-play hands on the river, or fold them, will become clearer as you gain experience.

Whether or not you make a call on the river depends entirely on how you read the situation. Reads, reads, reads, and a little "pot odds" math should be your guide. (I showed you how to calculate the pot odds earlier, on pages 81–82.) Only through practice will you be able to make good decisions on the end. Pay attention to how often you're right and how often you're wrong with your calls on the river. Was there a good reason that you called? Did you read your opponents well? Keep in mind that the idea is to constantly improve your reading skills along the way.

Five

LIMIT HOLD'EM: ADVANCED STRATEGY

Take note: because the concepts presented in this chapter are both subtle and complex, the beginning or intermediate player really shouldn't race right out to try them in serious games. Successful application of these concepts involves not merely knowing and understanding them but possessing the judgment to know how and when to apply them.

Your typical megalomaniac player (a jackal type) may well appreciate advanced limit Hold'em theory more than most of the rest of us. Which is to say, when using advanced limit Hold'em theory, you can often find yourself skating on very thin ice. Pursuing play in this fashion is often thrilling and dangerous, both to the user's opponents and to the user himself!

In this chapter I'll show you how to reraise opponents who are stealing blinds. Essentially, I'll teach you to steal from the stealers! You won't quite be Robin Hood, because while you'll be stealing from the rich, you won't be giving the plunder to the poor: you'll be adding it to your own stack.

We will also talk about adding "suited connectors" like 8d-9d, 4s-5s, and 6c-7c to the mix of hands that you can play before the flop. We'll talk about reraising people with nothing, in order to bluff them out. We'll talk about trapping and check-raising opponents, and more.

In this chapter you will learn:

- ➢ How to play suited connectors.
- ➢ How to use suited connectors to "advertise."
- ➢ The "fire up the table" strategy applied by Spencer Ouren.
- ➢ How to steal from the blind stealers.
- ➢ How to trap with big hands: the John Bonetti story.
- ➢ How to play advanced Hold'em on the flop: anything goes!
- ➢ Having position is always good.

All these advanced concepts should be used with great caution. Most of them shouldn't be used by anyone other than the top pros, because most of them are highly "read-dependent." In other words, when you've advanced to the stage of your poker career when you're able to read your opponents well, then your chances of using these concepts successfully will be greater.

PLAYING SUITED CONNECTORS

Now that we're contemplating advanced play, we'll add suited connectors to the mix of hands that you'll sometimes play before the flop. Notice that I said "sometimes." There is very little advice in the way of "always" or "never" when one reaches the advanced strategy concepts in Hold'em.

Generally, in order to play suited connectors, you need to have multiway action (at least three players in the pot). Generally, you don't want to call three bets with these types of hands. Nor do you want to play these kinds of hands too often. The best time to consider playing suited connectors is when you decide to reraise (three-bet) someone you feel is weak, before the flop, in the hope that you'll be taking the pot away from this player later in the hand. Stealing the pot with these suited connectors is quite similar to the concept of stealing from the blind stealers.

The problem with playing suited connectors is

that they don't win the pot very often. You might, for example, play 7d-8d or 9s-10s and hit a hand that will just get you into a lot of trouble. You might make top pair or second pair or even a flush and still lose a big pot. So the best way to play these kinds of hands is very carefully! If you're an advanced player, you understand that it's very difficult to fold the 7d-8d when the flop comes down 2-6-7. If you're trying to play suited connectors, you have to learn how to fold them at the right time. This takes finesse, skill, and, above all, reading ability.

Three Limit Hold'em Situations Appropriate for Playing Suited Connectors

SITUATION 1: One situation conducive to playing these hands is when someone has raised and two or three players have already called in front of me. Here I'm investing two bets with at least three other opponents. In this situation, I like to have at least 5-6 suited or higher. I don't see much value in 2-3, 3-4, or 4-5 suited: the pairs, straights, and flushes these hands might make are all too low. To show you what I mean, if I'm playing a hand like 3-4 suited, I'm hoping to make a straight. It's not that I object to making a flush, but mine would be the worst possible flush, and I could easily lose to a higher flush. So I'd rather make a straight, but unless I hit the hand absolutely perfectly with A-2-5, my straight is probably going to be on the low side of what's available.

For example, if the flop comes 5-6-7, I have indeed made my straight, but I'm vulnerable to people who are playing higher suited connectors: 8-9 just buries me, 7-8 gives my opponent top pair with an open-ended straight draw that can easily beat me, and both 5-6 and 6-7 leave me vulnerable to losing to a full house. Someone with pocket eights will be trouble too. But if my suited connectors are a little higher, I'm not quite as vulnerable to losing a big pot. I'm not going to hit a suited connector hand too often anyway, and when I do hit it, I want to be reasonably sure I'm going to win with it.

Playing suited connectors, I'm hoping to hit the flop pretty solidly; if I don't, I just surrender my two previous bets on the flop and fold the hand. I'm also prepared to jam the flop if I think I've flopped the best hand, in order to protect it.

SITUATION 2: The second favorable situation arises when I have suited connectors in the blinds, because I get in for a discount. In other words, calling two bets in the big blind amounts to calling just one bet, since it was I who posted the first bet in the blind.

SITUATION 3: The third situation involves messing with other players' heads and making myself more unpredictable in other players' eyes. In this situation, I'll make it three bets over the top of someone who I think is raising the pot with a weak hand in front of me. I may three-bet (reraise) a jackal when I'm on the button with 5d-6d in order to try to steal the pot from him.

If I *am* able to take the pot away, by forcing everyone to fold, then I'll just place my winning hand facedown. But if I get caught bluffing, then I'm more than happy to show the whole table my hand and say, "Six high." When the other players realize that I reraised with 5d-6d before the flop, then I can expect to receive a lot of extra action for a while! After I've shown down six high once or twice, then it's time to play the top ten hands only for a while, and wait for the players to give me their chips. They'll still be thinking that I have nothing (six high!), but I'll be showing them some real hands for a while. This pattern tends to keep many players off balance, and eventually they may decide they don't want to mess with me.

Calling with Suited Connectors

The idea behind calling two bets with suited connectors is to try to win a big pot. So I'm looking for a lot of opponents when I consider calling two bets with this hand. It doesn't make sense to me to call two bets with 8h-9h when no one else has called before the flop. In other words, I'm looking for good pot odds for this type of drawing hand. An occasional big pot pays for a lot of failed attempts.

Suppose that someone raises before the flop in early position and now two other people call the raise in front of me. I'm on the button with 4d-5d. I simply fold this hand, because 4-5 is below the suited connector line that I like to maintain. In this same situation, if I have 7-8 suited, then I'll go ahead and call the raise, trying to get lucky on the flop or later.

Suppose that a mouse in early position makes it two bets to go and now two other players call the two bets in front of me. I'm on the button with 9c-10c. In this case, although two other players have already called the raise, I'll probably fold my hand because the original raiser is a mouse. (When a mouse raises in early position, I'm always looking for an excuse to fold as soon as possible!) Of course, if the original raiser isn't a mouse, I would call with my 9c-10c. My rule for playing suited connectors is this: if two other people have called two bets (a raise), then I'll call with my hand (assuming that it's above the 4-5 line).

Calling with Suited Connectors in the Blinds

Usually, I will call two bets in the big blind with any suited connectors, even the weak ones like 2-3. After all, in the big blind it will cost me only one more bet to call, since I have posted one bet already. In the small blind, too, I will defend with most suited connectors, but I'll usually draw the line at 4-5 suited because it will probably cost me $1\frac{1}{2}$ bets more to call the two bets in the small blind. With 10-J or J-Q suited, I'm usually willing to call three bets in the blinds.

If I have 6-7 suited in the big blind and a mouse has made it two bets to go, then I will call if at least one other opponent calls, and I may call if I'm the only one left in the pot. Although I don't like to mess with a mouse's raise, the 6-7 suited in the big blind may bring a big reward for me if I hit the flop, and of course it will cost me only one more bet to see if I hit it. Moreover, a mouse is generally easy to read: he probably has a big pair or A-K high when he raises before the flop.

By risking one more bet to call before the flop, I may win a lot of bets from the mouse. And if I run into a troublesome flop like 10-6-4, then I can usually figure out fairly easily whether the mouse has me beaten or not. Again, in general I don't like to mess with a mouse's preflop raise, but being in the big blind (a discount) with suited connected cards is the time and place to do it.

If I have *any* suited connected hand in the big blind before the flop, then I'll call someone's raise (two-bet), period.

If I have J-Q or 10-J suited (they're both worth about the same before the flop) in the blinds, then I will in general call three bets (a reraise) before the flop. Of course there are exceptions: a mouse's three bets will force me to lay down my hand for sure! I have learned that it's very hard to beat Q-Q, K-K, A-A, or A-K with Q-J or 10-J suited! Use your own discretion when you're deciding to call three bets with J-Q or 10-J suited in the small blind. If you have a bad feeling that the three-bettor has a big pair, then just throw your hand away before the flop. Remember, you're getting only a half-bet discount, not much compared with the 2½ bets you would need to add, and you'll be playing the hand out of position for every betting round. The same thing applies to Q-J or 10-J suited in the big blind, although calling isn't ever a terrible play unless it's against someone who is a consistent mouse.

Three-Betting with Suited Connectors: Messing with the Other Players' Heads

It's time now to talk about advertising—a way of messing with players' heads in order to confuse them and induce action later on: three-betting someone with a suited connected hand like 6-7 suited. Why suited connectors? A suited connector is the kind of hand that you might hit easily when you're out there making a play. It's said that timing is everything in life, so how do you time this crazy move?

Before I go any further, I want to stress that it is a play you shouldn't use too often, and, further, that it's important to use this play against the right people. I would never use it on a mouse, for two reasons. First, the mouse is set in his ways and won't give you any extra action no matter what you do. Second, why take 6-7 suited against a big pair (which is probably what he has), when it's so hard to win that pot? Early in the evening is the perfect time and situation to use this play, because then you may get extra action all night long! Why use it when only a few more hands are to be played, when you won't gain the benefit of extra action?

In general, three-betting an opponent with suited connectors is a losing play for that one hand, but you make the play occasionally anyway because it will bring you extra action for another hour or two. This extra action will ultimately bring you more money, but it may also cause you to lose some pots that you ordinarily would have won when someone who now thinks you might be in there with any piece of junk runs you down with a really weak hand. Still, reraising with this type of hand will mess up the other players' attempts to read you. In the future when you three-bet preflop, they will begin to wonder whether you have 6-7 suited.

If you win one of these pots without having to show down your hand, then I recommend folding your hand facedown and trying the same play again soon. As long as the play keeps working and you don't have to show your hand, continue to use it. But when you've been caught bluffing with one of these hands on the end, then flip it faceup and say, "I have nothing." Even better is when you do hit your hand and flip it up at the end of the hand and say, "I have a straight!" It's pretty funny to watch the players at the table study your hand and realize that you three-bet before the flop with your 8-9 suited! When you show down weak suited connectors that you three-bet preflop, make sure that you're ready to play really tight for a while, since you will get extra action for a time afterward. Just make sure that you have a strong hand when they do call you down later.

Suppose that you're about one hour into a poker game that figures to last six hours or so. You have 8d-9d in late position and a jackal has just made it two bets in front of you. You now decide to make it three bets, and everyone folds except the jackal. The flop comes down Ah-Ks-4d, and the jackal bets out into you. Of course, you now go ahead and raise the jackal on the flop, attempting to take the pot away from him right then and there. If the jackal folds, just throw your hand away facedown. But if he calls, make sure that you try to bluff him on fourth street and the river. If he calls you down, then say, "Nine high" and flip your hand faceup. Just the look of the other players at the table will be worth the money that you lost on this hand! Well, maybe not just the look, but the look combined with the advertising is welcome! If the jackal folds his hand at some point, then fold your own hand facedown and try the same play again soon.

Suppose that the jackal calls preflop and the flop is 6h-7h-2s (assume that you've three-bet him preflop with 8d-9d). This is a great flop for you because if you hit a five or a ten you make a straight, and if you hit an eight or a nine you've made a pair of eights or nines, which would be top pair on the board. Of course you need to play this hand aggressively (ram and jam), and whether you

hit the winning hand or miss your hand, just flip it
faceup on the end when the jackal calls you down.
Obviously, it works out pretty well for you when
you do win the pot while making your "suited-
connectors three-bet advertising play." Just
remember that advertising is usually pretty
expensive, so make sure to look for ways to make it
pay big dividends. And don't advertise too often.

SPENCER'S APPROACH: "FIRE UP THE GAME"

Some years ago at the Bicycle Club Casino in Los
Angeles, there was a regular named Spencer
Ouren (he was very well liked). Spencer was about
my age and was on his way to becoming a poker
legend before his untimely death in 1992. Spencer
would sit down at the $80–$160-limit Hold'em
table and raise every hand *in the dark* to the maximum before the flop (he wouldn't even look at his
hole cards!) for one round. He did this every single
time he sat down in a high-limit game.

Players began to expect this seemingly suicidal
move, and some of them would decide to reraise
Spencer with a weaker hand than they would
usually play. Others, realizing what was happening,
would then call three bets with weaker hands than

they would normally play. Before long, all those in the game were caught up in playing hands that they didn't normally play. Spencer would thereby open up the game every time he sat down to play in it! Imagine what would happen. Often, the game might not have even been worth playing in before Spencer sat down, because everyone was playing tight (like a mouse). Then out of nowhere, Spencer sits down and all this craziness begins!

The players at the table would be playing hands that they didn't normally play for large amounts of money preflop. Invariably, some players would lose big pots with big pocket pairs like Q-Q, K-K, or A-A. Some of these players would then "go on tilt" and begin to play outside their normal, more successful style of play. Spencer was very good at shaking up a game by giving everyone a lot of action in the first round of play.

Usually, playing this way is a losing proposition, but because everyone knew what was coming (and then began to play out of character), if Spencer could win just one pot, he stood a good chance of losing only a little bit for the whole round. After all, these were pretty huge pots for the first round of deals he sat in! If he won just two pots, then he'd win (or break even) for the round. In any case, Spencer would then settle down after his "cap it in the dark" round and play supertight for a couple of hours afterward.

Invariably, the other players would continue to give Spencer too much action, and he was very successful because of this. His unique brand of firing up the table—thus messing with the other players' heads—by giving them a ton of action for one round is something worth looking into for even the greatest players in the world today. Sometimes, it would be a pretty expensive round for Spencer, but he would calmly sit back and take his $3,500 "start-up-cost" loss, knowing that everyone was now perfectly set up to be crushed for a couple of hours.

Spencer was thus a real master at "advertising" that he played weak hands. Usually, advertising costs money, but every marketing department in the world will tell you that well-placed advertising eventually pays big dividends!

STEALING FROM THE BLIND STEALERS

Stealing from the blind stealers is a very advanced Hold'em play. I'm not sure that it's a winning play, but it definitely falls into the realm of advanced Hold'em play. Personally, I like reraising players whom I suspect of stealing the blinds with a hand like any two cards ten and above (called "20" in honor of its value in blackjack), such as 10-K or 10-Q. I also like reraising with any ace. This play is a lot more effective if you reraise in a better position than the original raiser. (If the raiser is two or three off the button, then being on the button—and acting behind the raiser—gives you an edge, because you act last.)

Reraising with 20 is a lot more solid than just reraising with 5-7 off suit, because you have a playable hand when you get called (and everyone will call one more bet when he's already made it two bets). Nonetheless, it is important to talk about stealing from the blind stealers with a really weak hand. I know of a couple of world-class limit Hold'em players who absolutely love to reraise the "live" (weak) player in the game with nothing at all in their hand, in order to steal the pot from him or outplay him later on in the hand. This reraise of the live player in the game also causes them to isolate themselves (get it down to just the two of them) against the live player because the reraise usually drives the other players out of the pot. So the reraise (three-bet) of the live player isolates that player and gives the better player a chance to outplay him later on in the hand. And when you give this kind of extra action to the live player, he also gives you extra action, and believe me, he's the fellow you want extra action from!

A lot of good things can happen when you reraise the blind stealers preflop. If the blind stealer misses his hand (and remember, it's hard to hit a hand in Hold'em—you miss many more flops than you hit), then he'll often have to surrender his hand on the flop. You can also get lucky and win a big pot when you hit your own hand restealing.

On the other side of the ledger, you can get yourself in a heap of trouble making a three-bet resteal with a weak hand. If the alleged thief has your hand beat, you've already put in three bets to little purpose when you were losing, and he still has both position (when you reraise out of the blinds) and just as good a chance as you do to hit something on the flop. It just seems counterintuitive that you should be putting in three bets with 5-7 just because you suspect that someone is making a blind steal. Why not wait for a decent hand, one that is probably the best hand at the table preflop, before you three-bet it? This play may work best of all late in a Hold'em tournament when your opponent is more likely to throw his hand away on the flop, rather than risk going broke with a weak hand on the flop. (If I seem to be sending mixed signals, that's just poker; some advice is reliable, some is a crapshoot.)

TRAPPING WITH BIG HANDS
BEFORE THE FLOP

We have already talked about trapping players on the flop. I've seen my good friend John Bonetti, a world-class poker player at the age of 73, trap players before the flop beautifully! In 1996, in one memorable hand in the World Series of Poker championship event, John decided to try to trap the defending world champion, Dan Harrington, when there were still about 25 players left.

Dan opened the pot for $6,000 with Ks-10s, and John smooth-called the $6,000 bet with A-A. The flop was 6-9-10, and Dan bet out $25,000 into John. John again just smooth-called the $25,000 bet. I've got to tell you, I would have had to raise Dan's last $100,000 right there. I mean, I understand the smooth-call before the flop, though I rarely do that myself, but no way would I have just called the $25,000 bet on the flop! I would have been too scared that Dan had a pocket pair and would hit it for a set, just because I smooth-called his $25,000 bet instead of moving him all-in right there and then. The next card was an ace, for 6-9-10-A, and now Dan moved all-in for his last $100,000. John called Dan's $100,000 bet so quickly it gave me chills!

Then John looked up at me and winked. I was watching the action from about 20 feet away from the table and I had 50 percent of John that year (I had purchased 50 percent of his action). Having a piece of a player (sharing his wins and his losses) is often more brutal than being there at the table yourself, because you have no control over what's happening. Worse, first place was $1 million, which means I could have won $500,000 for my half! But I knew it was OK when John looked up and winked at me, and I wandered over to the table to see the upturned hands. Three aces for John and one pair of tens for Dan. John had had him drawing dead! No matter what the last card was, John would win the pot!

In this case, John had trapped Dan at just the right time. Sometimes traps trap the user, of course, but this one worked out perfectly. By the way, John went on to finish third that year, when the young and talented Huck Seed took first place. Having my two best friends at the time finish first and third was awfully cool. With John's second-place finish in the second-to-last event (for $140,000) and his third-place take in the main event ($680,000), we walked away with over $400,000 each! I always tell my poker friends when they visit my house, "This is the house that Bonetti bought!"

A good time to trap is when you are sitting in late position with A-A or K-K and you suspect that both blinds will fold if you make it two bets to go. By just calling the one bet, you allow the players behind you to call before the flop. By slow-playing with A-A or K-K and looking for action, you'll often get it. Sometimes, you need to be careful what you ask for! You may let the big blind play his 2-6 off-suit hand free by not raising before the flop, and then the flop may come 2-2-J and you are stuck in there losing a lot of bets because you trapped yourself. Still, sometimes I like to trap in this situation, and it usually works out pretty well for me (it's pretty tough to beat pocket aces or kings).

ADVANCED HOLD'EM ON THE FLOP

Advanced Hold'em on the flop is really all about reading other players. If you read your opponent as weak and think you might be able to take the pot away from him, then do it! If you have flopped a big hand and you feel that betting will drive out your opponent when what you want to do is keep him in the pot, then go ahead and trap your opponent by checking on the flop. Use your reading ability on the flop to determine what you can and cannot do. You may have flopped top pair, but if you read that your opponent has you beat, just fold your hand, having lost the minimum number of bets. If you read your opponent as being weak before the flop and you are making a steal on him, then make sure that you follow through on your steal attempt, unless you then have a strong read that he has hit the flop well. Again, advanced Hold'em on the flop is all about reading your opponents.

I know I keep mentioning reading the opposition, and I can't teach you how to be intuitive. I can, however, tell you that a lot of the information going into my reads comes from working hard at studying my opponents, both when I'm in a hand with them and when I'm out. Intuition springs from a combination of matters that you can understand and explain, and others that you can't. In the discussion of no-limit and pot-limit Hold'em (Chapter 6) I talk about a game I play while I'm at the poker table. The object is to try to determine someone's exact two hole cards in a hand. Through practicing guessing at what my opponent's cards are, even when I'm out of a hand, I increase my own reading abilities. (Flip on over to the material on no-limit for more details.)

Suppose that you have K-K before the flop and two opponents are also in the pot. If the flop comes down A-7-2, the advanced player makes his money by knowing what to do, on the strength of his read of his opponents. Does either of your opponents, or do both of them, hold an ace, a set of sevens, or a set of twos? How does the betting on the flop come down? Are your opponents capable of raising on the flop with just a pair of sevens or worse? If it does come bet and raised to you in this spot, will you three-bet it or fold? Odds are that you probably have to fold in this case, but what does intuition tell you to do?

I have played with advanced players who have bet out 8-8 on the end with a board of A-Q-7-5-3, simply because they thought they had the best hand, and they proved to be right! In fact, their bet was called on the end by someone who couldn't beat the 8-8! How did they know that the 8-8 was the best hand? How could they possibly have value-bet their hand in this case? Perhaps they knew that their opponent would never check a queen or an ace to them. In advanced Hold'em play on the flop, anything goes! As you try different things, you will find that the basic top ten strategy is a pretty good way to play Hold'em, with a twist—some well-timed intermediate and advanced moves along the way. The jackal lives in the advanced, wild, dangerous realm all the time, but it's very difficult to win when you play this way time in and time out.

DANGERS OF RESTEALS AND SUITED CONNECTORS

I'm not going to spend any more time in the realm of restealing and suited connectors in Hold'em, because it really is for expert players only, and it isn't to be dabbled in lightly! I would recommend that all beginners stay away from this advanced strategy, since they will find it very hazardous to their bank balances, with one exception: the suited-connector reraise (advertising) before the flop once or twice a night. I think this play is good even for a beginner, because it makes him more difficult for the rest of the table to read.

The real problem with advanced play—for all of us, whether we are world-class or beginners—is that it causes us to play too many hands. When we begin to win pots with 7d-8d (or see other players win with this hand), then we start to play 7-8 suited far too often before the flop. Pretty soon, 6-8 suited looks good as well. Playing suited connectors is like eating potato chips: once you eat one chip, you can't help eating many more! Once you start to win with suited connectors, you begin to play them all the time. I've seen people think this way many times in the past, "Three bets to me when I have 9d-10d; sure, I'll call. Why not, when I've been winning with these types of hands all night?" Beware of overplaying suited connectors. If you're not careful, before long you'll tell someone, "Man, was I unlucky with 6s-7s today. I called three bets and the flop was 8-9-10, and then..." Buddy, if you called three bets with 6s-7s, then you got what you deserved!

POSITION IN ADVANCED PLAY

Note that most of the plays I have talked about involve having the advantage of position. Being able to act last is a huge advantage in all forms of Hold'em. Imagine, you can just sit back and wait for all your opponents to act in front of you. "Just sit back and all will be revealed to you" isn't exactly the case, but it is nice to know where the other players stand. If the others check, then they're generally weak. If you have a powerful hand, then you can raise it when they bet. If you have a weak hand, then you can check behind them when they check. Having position in Hold'em is always good.

Six

NO-LIMIT AND POT-LIMIT HOLD'EM STRATEGY

It's time now to talk about the Cadillac of all poker games, no-limit Hold'em (NLH), and its brother, pot-limit Hold'em (PLH). In NLH you can bet any amount of the money in front of you on the table at any time! Imagine this concept: any amount at any time. If you sense weakness in your opponent, then go ahead and bet $100,000 on a pure bluff. Of course, if you bluff $100,000 at someone who has only $50,000 left in front of him on the table, then he is allowed to call for his $50,000, making your bet effectively $50,000. If we didn't have that protection in place, whereby you can bet only as much as your opponents have in front of them (called "table stakes"), then Bill

Gates would win every pot! Bluffing is a much bigger part of NLH and PLH than it is in limit Hold'em. The great bluffs, the great "reads," and the massive amount of strategy involved in NLH make it the most interesting and most strategically challenging game that we have in poker.

PLH is similar to NLH after the flop play, because by that point the pot in a PLH game has usually grown large enough to make huge bets possible. Before the flop, there are a fair number of strategic differences between the two games, because big bets aren't possible immediately in PLH. But in most respects PLH and NLH are roughly the same game.

In this chapter you will learn:

➢ The difference between no-limit Hold'em (NLH) and pot-limit Hold'em (PLH).
➢ How to introduce NLH into your home game—using "cash downs" to prevent runaway blowouts.
➢ Phil's "NLH fifteen" top hands.
➢ How to trap with A-A and K-K.
➢ Three theories on how to play pocket 2-2 to 8-8, and A-Q.
➢ Phil's game—"Guess your opponent's exact two hole cards."

> Phil's NLH theory.
> The "bet it all" NLH strategy—yuck!
> The "suited-connector" NLH theory that Huck Seed uses.
> The superadvanced "calling with nothing" NLH theory.
> Dave "Devilfish" Ulliott's NLH theory.

POT-LIMIT HOLD'EM (PLH)

In PLH you'll often be able to look at a flop, because the preflop raises are limited to the size of the pot. In fact, all bets are limited to the size of the pot. So, if the blinds are $1–$2, then the first raiser can only make it $7 to go: $1SB + $2BB + $2 call = $5 raise, so $2 call + $5 raise = $7 to go. (SB is small blind; BB is big blind.) If you've got $200 in front of you, wouldn't you like to take a $7 flop with a pocket pair? If you hit a set, then you may be a huge favorite and may get the other $193 into the pot. Let's take this example further and suppose that someone did open for $7 and two players called the $7, one of them the big blind. How much can then be bet on the flop? Well, $7 from the raiser + $7 caller + $1SB + $7BB (caller) = $22. Suppose that the big blind bets out the maximum $22. How much can the original raiser make it? Well, $22 in the pot + $22BB pot-size bet + $22 pot-size call from the raiser (he has to count his own $22 call before he makes a raise) = $66. So the original raiser can call $22 and raise $66, making it a total of $88 to go. The betting can escalate quickly in PLH.

Some world-class players believe that there is more skill in PLH than in NLH because there is more play on the flop in PLH. I believe that it is very close, but I will say that playing flops takes a ton of skill. The way some players play NLH today, folding or betting it all before the flop—without ever taking a flop—does take some edge away from the more skilled Hold'em players.

THE BIGGEST AND MOST PRESTIGIOUS POKER GAME: NO-LIMIT HOLD'EM (NLH)

Of the ten most prestigious poker tournaments today, six are NLH. The biggest two—the World Series of Poker (WSOP) and the World Poker Tour's Championship—each pay roughly $5 million for first place!

Imagine the scene in 2001 at the World Series of Poker when we were down to six players left in the tournament. I was still playing. The Travel Channel had a battery of cameras covering the table and the surrounding standing-room-only crowd. (Most of the crowd had to watch the action on television monitors set up throughout the room.) Two live Internet broadcasts were going on, one at my site (philhellmuth.com) and one at Mark and Tina Napolitano's site (PokerPages.com). With a first-place prize of $1.5 million and $6,130,000 in tournament chips lying on the table, we engaged in some pretty spectacular clashes that day.

In one hand, I opened the pot for $90,000 on the button with 9c-9s (exactly the same two cards that I won the WSOP with in 1989!) and Phil Gordon moved all-in in the big blind for about $550,000 total. I called his $450,000 raise so quickly that I freaked out everyone at the table! I just knew that he was going to move all-in with a weak hand, and I was ready for him. It turned out that he had 6-6, which made me a 4½-to-1 favorite to win the $1.1 million pot and bust him (I still had $500,000 in chips left if he won).

Unfortunately for me, the flop was 6-8-K, and his three sixes wound up winning the pot. If I had won this pot, then I would have had at least $1.6 million in chips and perhaps would have won my second "big one." My friend Andy, reading this book in draft, remarked that there's very little "perhaps" to it, although he was extraordinarily impressed with Dewey Tomko's play at the final table (Tomko finished second). Oh, well, either way, it was an exciting hand to be a part of! The two black nines lost the $1.1 million pot, but in 1989 they had held up for a $1.2 million pot and given me the WSOP title. So, 9c-9s is still my favorite hand, and I'd had a really good chance to immortalize it that day. Winning the most prestigious NLH event in the world is the best way to achieve poker immortality!

INTRODUCING NO-LIMIT HOLD'EM TO YOUR HOME GAME

Now is the time to tell you that if you introduce NLH to your own home poker game, watch out! The money won and lost can escalate pretty quickly. Before long, the size of the pots will be more than you bargained for. As a brake against this tendency I recommend that you introduce NLH in a "cash-down" format, which allows people to take a portion of their chips off the table at a certain predetermined chip total.

For example, you could require everyone to keep at least $50 in chips in play (making that the maximum they could lose in one pot), but allow them to take off the money above that amount. If someone wins a $110 pot, he can remove $60 in chips and put it in his pocket while keeping $50 in play in front of himself. In this way, the stakes won't go up and up and up after a few hours of NLH play, as they usually do.

This system also allows the players to play an amount they feel comfortable with. You might have two business owners keeping $2,000 apiece in front of themselves, and a couple of other players with only $70 each in front of themselves. It's also possible that one player has a mere $17 left, because he started with $50 but lost down to this point. How does the pot work if the two $2,000 players move all-in along with the $17 player on the same hand? The player with $17 is entitled to $17 each from the big stacks if he wins the pot. His money is matched by both opponents. In fact, the $17 player may well make a straight flush and lament the fact that he won only a $51 pot! Meanwhile, the nearly $4,000 side pot may be won by a player holding merely top pair! Ironically, the straight flush wins $51, but one pair wins a $3,949 side pot on the same hand.

If someone starts with $50, and loses $20 in one hand, then he can play the $30 until he goes broke. Again, the cash-down format also allows some of your richer friends ("big dogs") to leave a lot more money in front of them. So two of the big dogs could play as big a pot as they want to between themselves, while the little dogs have all-in protection for their money. *All-in protection* simply means that if you have $38 in front of you, then you can win all the money in front of each opponent up to $38 each (each opponent matches your $38). No matter what you saw in the entertaining but extremely inaccurate movie *Big Hand for the Little Lady*, in any poker game you can't be forced out of a pot because someone else has more money on the table than you do.

I believe that if you introduce NLH to your home game, the other players will love it, especially with the cash-down feature that keeps it under control. NLH is *the game* in the poker world right now. One reason is that it opens up poker and offers the possibility of making more challenging "moves." You can now make bluffs that have teeth. If you smell weakness in someone, you can raise him right out of the pot even if you're weak. You can now bet so much money on your drawing hand that you will force your opponent to fold! NLH is poker at its best, because you don't necessarily have to hold or make a lot of good hands to come out a winner. You can win pots with your reads and understanding of your opponents. It's a bit like playing chess with a sledgehammer!

The first thing that I'm going to give you in what follows is a base of hands that you can use when you play NLH. This starting base will include the top ten hands and the other pairs. Then I will expand this base somewhat to include A-x suited hands. Along the way I will talk about how some other top pros play these kinds of hands before the flop.

BEGINNERS' STRATEGY FOR NLH AND PLH

Even though there are some differences, I'm going to treat NLH and PLH as if they were the same game, for the duration of this discussion. As is always the case in Hold'em, supertight is right for beginning players while they learn to get their feet wet! Therefore I recommend that you restrict yourself to the "top ten hands" and pairs while you learn the game. In other words, play only the 13 pairs (aces down through deuces), plus A-K and A-Q before the flop in NLH. Although my top ten hands for limit Hold'em do not include the small pairs (2-2, 3-3, 4-4, 5-5, or 6-6), these pairs can win you far, far greater pots in NLH when you "flop a set" (hit three of a kind with them on the flop)—

much more often than you can win with them in limit poker. So my "NLH fifteen" are all the pairs, plus A-K and A-Q.

The idea behind playing only the NLH fifteen hands is that you will be playing hands that will win you big pots. These are the hands that you'll most often *double up* with: put your $210 into the pot and win a pot of $420+. The NLH fifteen strategy is very conservative but very effective against other beginners. To win NLH tournaments or larger NLH side games, you would need to play more types of hands, but here I'm addressing beginners' play.

The NLH fifteen strategy is simple. With these hands, you'll put yourself in some very good situations. You can double up when you flop a set. You can double up by getting your money into the pot with A-A, K-K, Q-Q, or A-K before the flop. You can even double up with 9-9, 10-10, or J-J, after the right kind of flop. The best thing about sticking to this strategy, at least in the near term, is that the game becomes easier when you play poker this tight.

Beginners: If You Hold A-A, K-K, Q-Q, or A-K Before the Flop, Bet It All

When you have one of these top four hands in NLH, you can almost always justify shoving all your chips out there before the flop. There are very few exceptions to this advice, and virtually no exceptions for the beginning NLH player. For the more sophisticated player, you will, once in a blue moon, be wise to fold Q-Q or A-K before the flop. If you're to do this, however, you should have some very strong evidence that your opponent holds K-K or A-A. The evidence might be that someone has made a big raise and then a mouse has moved all-in for a mountain of chips (for characterizations of my animal types—the mouse, elephant, lion, jackal, and eagle—see page 42 in Chapter 3). A mouse reraising someone with all his chips should set off an alarm or two in your head!

Beginners: Trapping with the Top Four Hands

The trapping theory for NLH applies mostly when you have A-A or K-K. Some players like to just call someone else's raise or reraise before the flop when holding A-A or K-K, in the hope that the move will trap someone into giving them all his chips after the flop. This is a dangerous theory, with a risk-reward hazard that any expert in game theory would love to look at! Most of the time you should just go ahead and reraise with A-A or K-K and hope that your opponent either moves all-in right there with a hand like J-J or Q-Q (which makes you a 4½-to-1 favorite) or folds his hand. Reraising is the safe way to play A-A and K-K; it prevents you from losing all your chips in some situations. You'll lose them all less often when you reraise with A-A or K-K, but you'll also usually get less action on these hands. When trapping works out, you look brilliant; but when you bust yourself trapping someone, you look like an idiot!

The trap works like a charm when you have A-A or K-K and your opponent has a hand like A-J, and the flop is 2s-2h-Jh. You may force your opponent with A-J into losing all his chips in this scenario because he may think you have K-J or a flush draw.

Trapping with aces can go badly for you, however, when your opponent hits his flop really well, as when he raises with Qd-Kd and you just call and the flop is K-Q-4: now you can kiss your chips good-bye. (However, think of the chips you'll win trapping with K-K on that same flop.)

Your trap could get uglier still if the raiser has 8c-9c, and now the flop is 5-6-7! In both these scenarios of trap gone bad, you would have won the pot had you reraised before the flop, but instead of winning the pot before the flop you have trapped yourself into losing all your chips! I rarely trap with any big hand, but some circumstances encourage me to try it. Trapping with aces is obviously safer than trapping with kings.

Beginners: Reraising J-J, 10-10, or 9-9 Before the Flop

J-J, 10-10, and 9-9 are strong NLH hands, and you should reraise with them when someone raises before the flop. With these three hands you really want to use the reraise to win the pot before the flop, because you're probably winning at that point and because these hands are very vulnerable to overcards on the flop. Sometimes, when you smell weakness in your opponents, you can make a stand with one of these three hands and put in all your chips. In general, though, you want to reraise someone else before the flop, and if he or someone else puts in another raise (a third raise) over the top of you, you should just throw your hand away. These three hands are usually in a lot of trouble when an opponent puts in the dreaded third raise! You're roughly a $4\frac{1}{2}$-to-1 underdog with an under-pair against an overpair in Hold'em. (The exact odds depend on which two pairs you're comparing, but $4\frac{1}{2}$-to-1 is close enough for most table estimations.)

Beginners: Pairs 8-8 and Under and A-Q— Three Different Theories

Let's examine three ways these eight hands (8-8, 7-7, 6-6, 5-5, 4-4, 3-3, 2-2, and A-Q) might be played in NLH. In my view, these small pairs and A-Q are the kinds of hands that you want to take a flop with; thus they are hands worth one raise before the flop, or even worth making the first raise yourself. If you're raising with one of these hands, then raise about the size of the pot (this is discussed above in PLH). So you can just make the first raise with one of these hands and, hopefully, win the pot when everyone folds before the flop. But you don't want to put in very much money with these kinds of hands before the flop. Ideally, you want to call a small raise (or the initial blind bet) or make a pot-size raise yourself before the flop, and then hit your hand on the flop (a set is a great hand) and win a huge pot! Again, my theory is that you want to call a small raise before the flop or make a pot-size raise before the flop to try to win the pot before the flop.

Frank Henderson's theory about this type of hand (Henderson is a noted player on the poker circuit) is to call one raise before the flop (on this much we agree). But Frank doesn't like to try to win the pot before the flop with these kinds of hands by raising the pot before the flop. Rather, he likes to just call before the flop and hope to win a big pot when he flops his set. So Frank wants to try to lose small with these hands when he misses them and win big if he hits them, by keeping other players in the pot before the flop. Actually, this theory sounds pretty good to me! The only downside is that he doesn't win as many pots before the flop. Maybe this is OK, because the pots you win with a raise before the flop tend to be pretty small anyway.

The megalomaniac theory of playing these types of hands is always to raise or reraise before the flop. Don't discount this "megalo" theory out of hand, because it works very well for a lot of players. These megalo players are superaggressive and will try to win every pot they play before the flop. If a megalo gets hold of some chips, he can make the other players at his table miserable with his constant raising and reraising. I would rather back a megalo player than a supertight player any day in an NLH tournament. The megalos tend to do well in NLH tournaments because they're always picking up chips; but in the side games they tend to get crushed, as the more patient pros sit back and wait for the megalos to overplay their hands against them. The reason why megalos do better in NLH tournaments than in the side games is that they steal a ton of antes in NLH tourneys.

So we have three different NLH theories as far as playing small pairs and A-Q are concerned. I rarely play the megalo theory, because my opponents expect me to play that way (sometimes you need to play that way if you are at a table full of mice). Rather, I play the theory I've laid out above, and I sometimes use Frank Henderson's theory as well. In other words, most of the time I will put in the first raise with these types of hands, but sometimes I'll just call with them before the flop.

INTERMEDIATE NLH THEORY: ADDING A-X SUITED

Now we'll simply add A-x suited to the mix of hands that you play. The ramifications of adding these hands are two: you can get yourself into trouble when you hit an ace or the x with an A-x suited hand, and you will occasionally make an ace-high flush.

Try not to lose too much money when you hit an ace with your A-x suited hand. In NLH most of the value of A-x suited comes when you hit the hand hard, as when you make a flush, two pair, or trips (when you make trips with the x card, it's hard for anyone to notice). When you hit the ace only, as with Ac-3c and a flop of A-K-2, then watch out! Don't get overinvolved in this situation, because anyone putting in big bets against you will almost certainly have you beat, unless he's bluffing. In limit Hold'em you can just call someone down in a situation like this, without doing too much damage to your chips, but in no-limit doing that could cost you a big chunk of your chips.

When you do hit your hand hard, then you need to figure out how to win the maximum number of chips with it. You should also be thinking about protecting your hand, especially when you draw a flop of 8c-8h-9c and you have As-8s. In this case, your opponents could be drawing to a straight or a flush. Keep this in mind when you think about betting a small amount to lure your opponents into the pot. The funny thing is that you want action with this hand and this flop, but you can't just let someone beat you for free. If you knew that your opponents didn't have a straight or a flush draw, then you could check on the flop, hoping for a lot of action on the next two rounds of betting. Betting out with a hand like this may cause someone with a drawing hand to raise you, and now you can reraise and win the pot right then and there.

GUESSING AN OPPONENT'S EXACT TWO HOLE CARDS

Ever since I started playing NLH I have incorporated a little game in which I try to guess exactly what two cards my opponent has in the hole. I can usually narrow it down to a very few possibilities, and on occasion I have ventured a guess out loud when I feel confident about it. Boy, did I freak the other players out when I would guess my main opponent's Q-Q and he would then flip his Q-Q faceup and say, "How in the world does he do that?"

How in the world *do* I do it? I'm able to do it because I practice observation, logic, and deductive reasoning while I play in the game. By the time someone has acted on his hand three or four times, a lot of information has been made available. How did he bet it before the flop? How much did he bet, and what did he seem to want his opponent to do in this hand? Did he look weak or strong? Exactly how weak or strong did he appear? What did he have the last time he acted this way? How did the flop alter his demeanor? Was he doing any acting that I could see right through? And of course the cards on the board figure heavily in my assessments.

Usually, all the information I gather in this way helps me form a mental picture of my opponent's hand. I'm blessed with an excellent poker memory as well (I still remember hands that I played 17 years ago, and all the details—not just hands of today or yesterday), and all that helps the process too. So I could narrow it down to, say, a pair of tens, jacks, or queens. Then I would think for another few seconds and refine my guess on the basis of the way my opponent had acted in the past during a hand that I witnessed. Finally, I would throw out my guess, "You have pocket queens in the hole, don't you?" I became so good at this little trick that for a long time the other players stopped trying to bluff me. (This was awfully nice for me, but on the other hand I wasn't picking off anyone else's bluffs either!)

Trying to determine the cards your opponent holds is a great game when you play poker, and it will help your reading skills immeasurably. If you're bad at it at first, don't worry—your reads will get better and better. Practice makes perfect! Daniel Goleman claims in his book *Emotional Intelligence* that "certain 'star qualities' are learnable." (Goleman believes that many of the characteristics that have made some people very successful can be studied and learned.) I believe that reading people is a learnable "star quality" (characteristic), although I concede that some people can take it further than others. In any case, you'll improve your reading skills a lot with practice. And when you're way off on a guess, you'll begin to see why. ("Oh yeah, I forgot that he reraised before the flop with that hand.")

JUDGMENT IS EVERYTHING IN NLH

In NLH all manner of plays are possible. You can fold K-K before the flop or move all-in with 2-7 off suit, bluffing before the flop, if your judgment is good enough. By the way, I've folded K-K before the flop only a few times in my life, and every time I did, I was right, because my opponent did indeed have A-A! One thing you'll learn as you play more poker is that when someone has the best possible hand, he is often easily readable.

Quiz show hosts like to say, when the pauses are too protracted, "Go with your first gut instinct. That first instinct is always right." You'll find yourself in a lot of interesting situations in NLH where your judgment and your guts will be severely tested. Whether or not you make the right decisions will go far toward determining whether or not you'll win for the day (it helps to have good cards too). You think that you're under pressure at work? I've seen players who have all their money in the world on the table call other players' bluffs for all *their* money. In other words, if they're wrong, then they're busted!

One excellent rule for NLH is this: if you can't allow yourself to fold the best hand, then you can't win. In many of the tournaments that I've won I've had occasion to fold the winning hand. In the World Championships in 1989, when just four players were left, I folded pocket tens before the flop against Johnny Chan's pocket nines in a big pot, but I still went on to win the tournament! It's not who wins the battle; it's who wins the war. Don't be afraid to fold your hand in NLH if you think that it's beaten. If it was the winner, so what? You made your decision, and you're still at the table with chips. Stay focused on winning, not on looking back at your untimely fold.

PHIL'S NLH STRATEGY

I like to take pieces of every different strategy I'll be laying out below and keep them in my arsenal for eventual use. I like to stick to a very tight beginner-type overall strategy, one involving playing very few hands for the most part. In this way, there isn't too much pressure on me to make tough decisions all the time. So most of the time in NLH I like to play only the "NLH fifteen" hands.

When someone behind me is playing too tightly, in NLH, I like to raise the pot to try to steal the blinds from him, whenever it's his big blind.

I trust my instincts when I'm deciding whether or not a player is bluffing. My poker instincts have been very, very good to me. I hone these instincts by practicing reading my opponents when I'm out of the hand being played, to try to get a better read on them for when I need it later. (In mentioning my own play I'm trying only to show you what's possible if you practice and develop your instincts.)

If someone has raised in front of me and I feel that he is weak, I usually fold anyway. But at the end of the hand I'll watch to see if he exposes his hole cards, so that I can confirm that he was weak or see that I was wrong. If I have confirmation that I was right, then I wait for him to do it again. Anyone who makes one weak raise can be expected to make more than one. When that player makes another raise and I feel it is weak, I go ahead and reraise him, to force him to fold his weak hand. This reraise wins many more chips than a mere blind steal would win, but you're also risking a lot more chips to win the pot when you reraise on a bluff.

Phil's Strategy: Reraise with Nothing

When I teach NLH theory in seminars, I like to use an example from the World Series of Poker (WSOP) in 2001. I had been watching Daniel Negreanu very closely during the championship event on day three. In this particular hand Daniel opened the pot for $10,000. I knew he had nothing, and when it was my turn to act I made it $30,000 to go with 10d-2d (bluffing). Now John "World" Hennigan decided to move all-in for $30,100, and Daniel quickly folded his hand. I called the $100 more, but I would have called another $10,000 because of the size of the pot (I had about $210,000 in front of me at the time). After all, I already had $30,000 in the pot plus John's $30,100 and Daniel's $10,000. Much to my embarrassment, the tournament director required us to flip our cards faceup before the flop. He wasn't picking on us; that's the rule at WSOP when one player is all-in. This is a new, controversial industrywide rule in poker in 2002, and the reason that it exists is to prevent collusion. Many of the top players hate this rule because it forces them to show their hands and therefore exposes their style of play. Now players get to see, free, what the great players are doing. ("He bet all his chips with that hand?")

When the hands were announced, a lot of snickering was heard from the crowd (how did Phil get $30,000 in before the flop with 10-2?), and most of the players left in the tournament came over to watch this pot. John had 9-9 and I had 10-2! Basically, I needed a ten to win. Anyway, the flop and the turn came 7-8-3-K, and then a ten hit on the last card! What a lucky card for me! I don't know what John was doing putting his last $30,000 into a pot when it was raised and reraised in front of him before the flop, and I didn't like his play at all. I hadn't been making any plays that day, and even if he suspected that I was making a play, pocket nines isn't a very good hand to make a stand with, especially given that he couldn't even raise me out of the pot. Also, John had to worry that Daniel would get involved in this pot, although Daniel was probably going to throw his hand away, facing both my raise and John's call. Still, there was some chance he was going to be facing two opponents, which meant that his 9-9 was just too vulnerable. More to the point, though, John had to figure he was going to be heads-up with me, and my reraise against Daniel should have meant strength to him.

Be that as it may, John's instinct was right, so I have to give him credit for his call, and perhaps for figuring out that Daniel and I were both bluffing! Anyway, here is an example of a pot that was won while someone was making a move. Daniel later admitted having six high in this hand (he folded his hand facedown because he didn't call the $30,100 bet).

If someone raises a very small amount before the flop (less than 5 percent of my chips), I will often call with suited connectors and take the flop. When I do this, I'm putting a lot of pressure on myself to read my opponents well. Sometimes it works out beautifully and I have a huge flop and win a big pot. Sometimes I have to scramble and make a great fold in order to save chips. Sometimes I bust myself because I can't get away from (can't fold) my hand after the flop.

I'm capable of trapping with big hands like a pair of tens, jacks, queens, kings, or aces, but I'm very careful that I don't trap myself with these hands! I rarely use this play, because it can be very dangerous in NLH.

I absolutely hate getting all my chips in with any hand. When you are all-in you can go broke! Of course, if I have the best possible hand on the last round of betting, then I love to get all my chips in. I try to avoid getting all-in in NLH unless it can't be helped.

More often than I probably should, I will throw away the best hand when I play NLH. I will throw away very strong hands if I believe that they're beaten, no matter how much money is already in the pot. When you can do this, you can escape losing situations and even consider that you've gained an emotional win. I folded pocket kings before the flop at the World Championships in 2001 when my opponent opened for $1,200, I reraised him to $3,800, and he then moved my last $12,000 all-in. I thought he had pocket aces, so I folded my hand, rather than risk my last $12,000. As he was throwing away his hand facedown, I said, "Show me pocket aces!" Amazingly, he did show them.

The next day I folded my A-6 hand after a lot of money went in before the flop and the flop came down Ac-10d-6d. My opponent could have had Ad-Qd or Ad-Kd, which would have given him a flush draw and top pair, but that would have made me and my two pair the winner. He told me later that he had As-10s, for two better pair than mine! Two days later I had more than $1 million in chips in front of me, and yet I would have been broke if I hadn't thrown away both those strong hands! The ability to throw away strong hands is a mark of an NLH champion.

I often protect my hands with huge bets and raises. At the preliminary NLH event at the WSOP that I won in 2001, I moved all-in with A-A after I was check-raised on a flop of Ad-6h-7s. Even though I had the best possible hand and had good reason to suspect that the opponent who had check-raised me on the flop was drawing dead (had no wins!), I decided that I didn't want to take a chance that my opponent might catch two perfect cards. This was the classic slow-play situation because we were the two chip leaders at the time. Instead of smooth-calling my opponent's $15,000 check-raise on the flop (as 98 percent of the pros in the world would do), I went ahead and raised him his last $50,000, and he threw his hand away. (Did I mention that I went on to win the tournament?) Perhaps if I had slow-played my hand, my opponent would have caught an eight and a nine to make a ten-high straight with his A-10 and a board of A-6-7-8-9.

In the World Championship event in 2001, faced with an $18,000 opening bet and a $70,000 raise to go, I moved all-in for more than $550,000 with my A-A, to send a message that I had A-A! A lot of players would have raised less, to lure their opponent in before the flop. By the way, I later did what's called *rabbit hunting*—looking at the deck after the hand is over, to see what would have happened had additional cards been dealt out—and discovered that the flop would have been K-2-3 had my opponent not folded his pocket K-K hand! I would have had one more *bad beat* (bad-luck) story to tell if I had only reraised a little bit or smooth-called his $70,000 bet. Of course, my opponent kept rabbit hunting, and he claims an ace was coming on the last card. (I didn't look beyond the flop!)

I will call someone on the end with ace high or worse if I think I have the best hand. I recently called a $30,000 bet from Carlos Mortensen (the WSOP champion in 2001) with K-Q high, and he had me beaten with a small pair.

I like to play conservatively and hang around in an NLH game or tournament until I smell blood or have a good situation come up for me. I wait for the chips to come to me. Eventually, my opponents start to make mistakes that I can take advantage of. When I feel the time is right, I will make some moves. I might call someone with a weak hand when he's bluffing, or I might bluff someone when I smell weakness. I may even try to trap someone if I make the nuts, but generally I bet the nuts to give someone a chance to break himself against me in a pot. In the hand I mentioned above, where I flopped a set of aces, I actually bet big on the flop before I was check-raised! Most players wouldn't dream of betting when they're heads-up with a set of aces but no draw is on the board. If my opponents are playing too tightly, I'll start to raise every pot to steal some chips, especially when there are antes to steal as well as blinds. (Antes aren't usually used in Hold'em, but they are added to Hold'em tournaments in later rounds and sometimes to high-limit side games.)

I play NLH by feel, with some discipline, to make sure I stay around for a while. And I trust my reading powers implicitly. If they punch, then I counterpunch. If they lower their guard, then I strike. I sit back and watch what others are doing, and then I make adjustments to my play. Sometimes I play my style, and other times I play a style based entirely on my opponents' styles.

The "Bet It All" Strategy for NLH—Yuck!

In the "bet it all" strategy you raise all your chips to open a pot or to reraise in a pot. So if the blinds are $10–$20 and it's your turn to act from late position in a hand, then you just go ahead and open for the whole $1,000 you have in front of you. You will win that $30 in blinds quite often when you bet $1,000, but you're risking $1,000 in order to win $30! You do the math! Actually, a lot of poker players use this crazy strategy these days. The downside is that you're risking all your chips, and if your opponent picks up a strong hand you'll lose the whole $1,000; and for what: $30 in blinds? If someone else opens a pot for $60, and the *slider* (he likes to slide all his chips in!) decides to play his hand, then he just bets it all. ("Your $60 and $940 more.") I think the main reason these players do this is that they're afraid to play their hands *after* the flop, although some of them just fail to understand the long-term implications of betting a lot in order to win a little.

The good side of betting it all is that it prevents someone with a marginal hand from raising or reraising you before the flop. Suppose that I have A-J on the button and now you raise it to $60 to go in late position. I may reraise you, thinking that you're weak because you raised the pot in late position ("He's just stealing the antes"), and therefore I think you're just trying to steal the blinds. If you have 10-10 and decide to reraise me as well, I may have to call you if I don't have a lot of chips left. Now we're going to play an even-money pot (actually, not quite even money, because the 10-10 is about a 13-to-10 favorite over the A-J), which the champion players like to avoid.

It's difficult to win consistently when you play a lot of coin-flip hands in a tournament! When you do bet it all before the flop, my only option left is to fold my marginal A-J.

For a while in the 1990s a lot of sliders reached the final tables at NLH events. Sliding all one's chips in is probably a good strategy for a weaker, inexperienced player. This way he will get lucky for a big pot or he will be eliminated, but at least the great players won't be able to slowly pick him apart. Still, for a good or great player, or someone aspiring to be a good or great player, anything that takes away your options in NLH is bad. Sliding a mountain all-in to try to win a molehill takes away all your options and is a very risky play as well. One bad move like this, and you find yourself out of options when the player behind you jumps up from his seat because he has pocket aces. It's too late now to take advantage of this new information, because you've already made your big move all-in!

HUCK SEED'S ADVANCED THEORY OF SUITED CONNECTORS FOR NLH

This suited-connectors theory is very advanced and could be dangerous to your bankroll's health. I call it "Huck Seed's" theory, but in fact I've used it myself in days past. And besides, to pigeonhole Huck Seed's great NLH play into this one theory would be unfair to Huck. Huck can play many different ways at different stages of a tournament or side game. Be that as it may, he often does play this theory successfully, as does the talented, young, up-and-coming Daniel Negreanu.

This is the theory of calling other players' raises with suited connectors, such as 6d-7d or 8c-9c or even 3s-4s. These are excellent drawing hands in NLH. Ideally, you want to call an opponent's $400 bet with a hand like 4d-5d when he has another $10,000 to $20,000 left in front of him. This way, if you hit your hand, you may win that other $10,000 to $20,000. So the idea is to call a small bet from your opponent and win a large stack of chips when you hit your hand.

Suited Connectors

Here is an actual hand that I saw, between Daniel Negreanu and a two-time world champion, Johnny Chan, at the Taj Mahal in Atlantic City in the $7,500 buy-in championship event in 1999. With the blinds at $400–$800 and more than $12,000 in front of him, Johnny opened the pot for $2,600 with A-K. Daniel called the $2,600 with 7s-9s, and the flop came down Ad-7d-7c. (Daniel flopped trip sevens!) Johnny bet out small ($2,000) on the flop, and Daniel raised small ($3,000). After studying things for a while, Johnny moved all-in and Daniel quickly said, "I call." Daniel wound up busting Johnny out on this hand; and Johnny, shocked, said to me a few minutes later when I approached to offer sympathy, "Can you believe this kid?" Here is a case where Daniel invested $2,600 to win more than $12,000 if he hit. The suited connectors worked like a charm.

The downside of playing like this, of course, is that you will put yourself in a lot of untenable situations. What are you going to do when the flop comes down 2-3-8 and you have 8c-9c? You have flopped top pair, which is fairly powerful, but what happens when your opponent has J-J in the hole? Answer: you may lose a lot of chips! In fact, if you're not careful, you can lose all your chips in this situation.

You can thus expect to have some severe chip swings when you play poker like this. When I watched Daniel use this approach in the world championship event in 2001, his chips were up to $450,000 (and the chip lead) and then down to $70,000 and then up to $700,000 (and the chip lead again!) and then down to $170,000! Up and down, up and down, so it went with Daniel at this

WSOP. He is a great NLH player, but these kinds of swings just can't be good.

Let's return to the example above for a moment. Why was Johnny shocked by Daniel's play in this example hand? Because Daniel risked almost 20 percent of his own chips before the flop with 7s-9s. This was just too high a percentage of his chips to risk with this hand. If you want to play this way, try not to risk more than 7 percent of your chips before the flop with these suited-connector hands.

Playing the suited connectors requires an excellent read of your opponents, so that you don't get yourself into trouble when you hit some of these hands halfway. Before you try this approach, make sure that you're reading your opponents almost perfectly. I would never recommend this theory to any novice or intermediate-level player!

When Suited Connectors Don't Work

In the main event at the WSOP of 2001, I made a raise of $3,000 with Kd-Jd and Daniel called me with 6d-5d. The flop was 10d-7s-2h, and I checked and then Daniel checked. The next card off was 9d, for 10d-7s-2h-9d, so that I now had a straight and a flush draw. Any diamond would make me a flush, and any queen or eight would make me a straight. I decided that I needed to make a big bet with this draw, since Daniel had checked the flop and I thought he was weak, so I bet out $10,000.

Meanwhile, Daniel had also turned a straight and a flush draw. Any diamond made him a flush, and an eight made him a straight. Little did he know that the diamond made me a higher flush and the eight made me a higher straight! Anyway, he called the $10,000 bet, not knowing that he really didn't want to hit his hand, because it would cost him another $20,000 if he did! The last card was a "blank" 3c, and now I checked and Daniel checked also, thinking that I was strong. I said, "You win it, I missed." He said, "No, you got it." At that point, I knew that my king high was good, and I flipped it faceup and collected the pot. Daniel said, "Whew, it's a good thing I missed my hand!" as he showed me his hole cards.

Why didn't I try to bluff Daniel on the end? For the same reason that he didn't try to bluff me on the end: we usually call each other when we have anything! And if he had tried to bluff me on the last round of betting, I might have just raised him if I noticed any weakness at all in his bet on the end.

This example illustrates another problem with suited connectors. You might just end up drawing to the lower straight or flush and wind up losing all your chips when you hit it!

SUPERADVANCED "MEGALOMANIAC" NLH THEORY: PLAYING WITH NOTHING

Some great NLH players like to call an opponent's raise with any two cards, because they think they can outplay the raiser later on in the hand. Again, I'll single out Daniel Negreanu as a player who uses this strategy. (Sorry, Danny.) In many NLH tournaments I've watched Daniel apply this strategy, knowing full well what he was doing! The key to the strategy lies in recognizing who the preflop raiser is. If the preflop raiser is a weak player (if you're new to the game, it's more fair to call you "inexperienced" than "weak"), look out for Daniel, because he'll be coming at you!

Many weaker or inexperienced players don't know how to bet or how to disguise their actions when they hit or miss the flop. They may, for example, jump out of their seats or bet in a very confident manner when they hit a flop. Conversely, they may telegraph their actions when they miss the flop, by betting with doubt or uncertainty written all over their faces. If they do hit, then Daniel folds (unless one of those "goofball" 6-8 off-suit hands of his actually hits). If they miss their hand, then Daniel bluffs them out and wins the pot. Of course, Daniel occasionally hurts his opponents or himself in a big pot when both he and his opponent hit the flop.

I give Daniel Negreanu and Huck Seed a lot of credit for being able to use this strategy successfully. Of course, if you ever travel the poker-tournament trails, you will see other top players, such as Layne Flack, Ted Forrest, Men Nguyen, and Amir Vahedi, using this dangerous strategy to good effect. But it is a bit too risky for my taste; I just don't like to be always putting a lot of pressure on myself to "read" my opponents and then fold my hands after I hit them on the flop. (Hitting a flop and then folding your hand because you read your opponent as being strong is a hard thing to do.) But someone who uses this theory well can accumulate a lot of chips very quickly!

DAVE "DEVILFISH" ULLIOTT'S THEORY OF NLH

The Devilfish is a great PLH and NLH player from Hull, in the United Kingdom. He has won PLH and NLH titles in the United States and Europe. Devilfish thrives on coming into a pot raising with almost anything before the flop. He may raise with 4-7 off suit or 2-5 off suit. He will almost always bet out at you on the flop, whether he misses the flop or hits it. This gives all the others a chance to fold their hands and gives Devilfish his second chance to win the pot with a bet or raise. (His first chance was before the flop with a raise.) He is very good at reading players, and that's one thing that all tough NLH strategies have in common. They all consider reading the other players well an essential ingredient.

If you do hit something and call Devilfish on the flop, then the pot has only just begun. If he thinks you'll fold your hand before risking a big bet on fourth street, then he'll bet big on fourth street, trying to bluff you. If he feels you'll fold your hand for an all-in bet, then he'll risk his whole tournament and bet it all. Likewise, he'll bet all your chips when he feels he has the best hand. This constant power-play pressure is also used by Men "The Master" Nguyen, Erik Seidel, Layne Flack, John Bonetti, and many other successful NLH tournament players. I used to use this approach myself, but once my opponents took to calling me down consistently, I began showing them only big hands. If they're going to call you, be ready to bust them.

If Devilfish wins a few pots before the flop, a few pots on the flop, and a few pots on the end with a bluff, he'll be way ahead of the game. This is a good theory of NLH play, but if used wrongly it can be disastrous for the player who is applying it. You can bluff at the wrong times and lose a lot of chips very quickly. As with all good NLH theories, if you use this one well you'll accumulate a lot of chips quickly, but if you use it badly you'll cough them up just as quickly.

DEVELOP YOUR OWN STYLE

What tactics should you adopt? My advice is to take a little bit from here and a little bit from there, and concoct your own style of NLH play. Some people try to play like me or Huck Seed or other great NLH players, such as T.J. Cloutier. This is usually a mistake, because those who attempt it are getting away from their own strengths, and they aren't far enough along in their own poker development to do all the things—simultaneously—that the great NLH players do. As you continue to develop your own style, get rid of the tendencies that don't work and add some of the traits that you see in the great players or read about here, but do it slowly! Make sure that a change in a move or a style works for you before you commit yourself to it for an extended period. Above all else, make sure that you're enjoying yourself when you play NLH. Otherwise, what's the point? Only a few players can count on making money over the long haul in this game, so you had better enjoy the journey!

To learn more about where and when the major NLH and PLH tournaments are played, go to philhellmuth.com or any one of these other sites:

- CardPlayer.com
- PokerPages.com
- LiveActionPoker.com.

Seven

LIMIT HOLD'EM TOURNAMENT STRATEGY

I wrote this in 2002; in 2004 the World Series of Poker had 2,600, yes 2,600, players! First place was $5 million, second place was $4.5 million, and third place was $2.5 million. In 2004, the World Poker Tour has come into its own, and playing the WPT events gets my juices flowing!!

I still love poker tournaments, even after playing in more than 900 of them in the 1990s alone; I enjoy every one that I play in. The event that really fires me up, though, is the World Series of Poker (WSOP). The WSOP is where legends and champions are made; it is the poker world's world championship.

In golf there are four major tournaments, but in poker the series of events constituting the WSOP carries so much prestige that it is in effect the U.S. Open, the Masters, the British Open, and the PGA all rolled into one!

With 643 players putting up $10,000 each for the WSOP championship event of 2002, creating a prize pool of $6.43 million, the money alone almost matched the prestige of winning the event. The investment banker Robert Varkonyi took home the first prize of $2 million; the second-place finisher, Julian Gardener, had to settle for only $1 million! For a lot of players, this is life-changing money, and so it isn't surprising that a lot of poker players covet the money more than the title. I'm not one of them: I love the title more than the money! The title brings with it a lifetime of recognition and prestige. The winner is forever called a world champion of poker, and his or her picture will go up on the Wall of Champions forever (at both of the Horseshoe Casinos, one in Las Vegas, the other in Tunica, Mississippi). You can see the Wall of Champions at PokerPages.com.

In 1970 Benny Binion started the WSOP, at his Horseshoe Casino in Las Vegas, and called it poker's world championships. It has been poker's world championship ever since, and it has grown in stature and popularity each year.

When you win the WSOP, you are no longer

just a poker player but rather a world champion. This distinction is nice, as my wife found out when she searched for residency programs back in the early 1990s. When asked about her husband's occupation, she would say, "He's a world champion of poker." I'm sure that this sounded more interesting and prestigious than "He's a professional poker player" or "He plays poker for a living!"

Every year in late April, the best poker players in the world (and a lot of wannabes) gather at the Horseshoe Casino in Las Vegas for roughly 25 to 33 WSOP events (the precise number changes from year to year), culminating in the "big one." The "big one" is the $10,000 buy-in Championship Event that ESPN, the Discovery Channel, the Travel Channel, and other television networks show up to cover every year. (ESPN now does 30 hours of adrenaline-pumping coverage of the WSOP each year.) The lowest buy-in event at the WSOP currently is set at $1,500. If you plan to attend the WSOP and play every event, make sure that you bring $100,000 with you! These 30 days (the "big one" alone is five days long) are undoubtedly the most exciting in poker, every year, and by far the most lucrative.

All champion poker players have to start somewhere, though. Learning to win limit Hold'em poker tournaments was very difficult for me. Even though I was already a world champion of poker and had won many big no-limit Hold'em events by the time I was 26 years old, I still hadn't even made my first final table (which is usually the final nine players) in a limit Hold'em tournament.

If you were a pro and I told you this, you would think it was really odd. How could I win so many no-limit Hold'em events but consistently have trouble making the final nine in limit Hold'em events? After a while, I began to realize that the way I was playing my hands was holding me back, so I did what I had never done before in poker: I studied a couple of other players to see what they were doing differently from me. Remember this the next time you start to blame your lack of success on bad luck: even a world champion was willing to admit he had things left to learn.

With no-limit, I could see what everyone else was doing wrong in the late 1980s. For some reason, the right way to play no-limit just seemed obvious and easy to me. Of course, I also did my fair share of playing no-limit Hold'em badly, but at least I knew when I was playing badly. (Moreover, that had to do with emotional issues, which I still struggle with at times, obviously!)

In this chapter you will learn:

➢ Aggressive play is right in limit Hold'em tournaments.
➢ Tight play is also right in limit Hold'em tournaments.
➢ Stealing blinds helps you survive *late* in limit Hold'em events.
➢ To win, steal more blinds at the money-cutoff line.
➢ Survive and thrive.
➢ Bring your big guns to a war!
➢ How to trap in limit Hold'em tourneys.
➢ Playing satellites improves your game.

AGGRESSIVE PLAY HELPS IN LIMIT HOLD'EM EVENTS

One day after I was eliminated from a limit Hold'em event, I sought out Jack Keller, who at the time was really hot in limit Hold'em tournaments, and watched him play for a couple of hours. It was obvious to me that Jack was doing a number of things I hadn't been doing. He simply tried to win every pot that he played. Jack never just called someone else's raise before the flop: he always either threw his hand away or three-bet it.

This was quite different from my old strategy. I

used to just call when I had a small pair, hoping that others would call as well, and that I would win a big pot when I finally hit my set. Jack, however, always three-bet before the flop, even with only a small pair, and continued to play his hand aggressively from that point on in the hand. The percentage of pots that he won was much higher than the percentage of pots that I had won, for three reasons.

First, Jack's constant three-betting before the flop helped him win more pots by eliminating more opponents preflop. When you start with fewer opponents before the flop, you'll win more pots.

Second, Jack would play his hand pretty hard on the flop and win a lot of pots if his opponents had, say, king high when an ace hit the board.

Third, Jack would just plain try to bluff you out if he thought he could.

This aggressive play of Hold'em hands is something I've already preached to you in earlier chapters of this book. Once I began using this system, I couldn't believe the results I achieved. I made five final tables in a row playing limit Hold'em this way, and eventually, in the 1990s, I won two world championships in limit Hold'em.

TIGHT PLAY HELPS IN LIMIT HOLD'EM EVENTS, ESPECIALLY EARLY

Tight play is also an important factor in success at tournaments. The really tight players tend to be around en masse fairly late in limit Hold'em events. These players tend to play almost as tight as the "top ten only" strategy (which I discuss in Chapter 3). Notice that I said these players were around, and not that they were winning the events. Although there are usually a ton of supertight players left late in a limit Hold'em event, they usually don't win the event or even make the final table. I believe that supertight play helps you last in limit Hold'em events, but you need to be able to change speeds at the right time if you're going to win some of them.

The right strategy against a group of supertight players differs from the right strategy against a group of average players. In fact, Jack Keller's three-betting preflop with every hand that he plays is more successful against a supertight player who will fold his hand right away if he misses it. Which tight player is going to win the pot when Jack three-bets his 5-5 into his 7-7? For example, when the flop comes A-J-2, then Jack can win pretty easily with a bet on the flop. Although supertight play will help you last, you will need to change your tactics at some point in order to win.

Therefore, I recommend playing the "top ten only" strategy for the first five or six hours of any Hold'em event while the weaker players are weeded out. After the first few hours of playing this strategy, it is time to switch tactics a bit.

STEALING THE BLINDS HELPS YOU SURVIVE LATE IN LIMIT HOLD'EM EVENTS

At some point after the first five or six hours, it's time to start stealing the blinds from the supertight players who are still alive in the tournament. But be wary of stealing the blinds from the looser players or the champion players, because they will probably defend with skill. Stay aware also of the person who keeps stealing your blinds, because at some point you will have to make a stand against that player.

If you take a close look around your table about six hours into the event, every time you enter one of these events, after a while you will develop the ability to see into the future a little bit. For example, there will probably be someone at your table who is playing way too loose but nonetheless is still alive. You may worry that this player may continue to be lucky, but chances are that he will bust himself out sooner rather than later, because of his reckless play. There will also be a player at your table whom you will recognize as being very tight, and you can figure that he or she will probably be around very late in the tournament, although probably low on chips.

You may even be able to see that the loose player is the one who may be your ticket to lasting another few hours yourself. Six or so hours into the event, with your blind-stealing working well, you need to make sure that you're still in a very tight mode of play. Surviving at this point in the tournament is the name of the game. But make sure that you're stealing blinds from the supertight players. (Don't worry; you will know who they are.)

STEAL BLINDS AT THE MONEY-CUTOFF LINE

When you start to reach the money-cutoff stage (when, say, there are 19 players left, and the tournament pays only 18 spots), make sure that you have your priorities straight. As the other players begin to play even tighter, in order to last until the final 27 or 18 players, you need to understand that making the money isn't your objective at this point. You are here to finish in the top three and make the big money.

One phenomenon you will observe is that when there are 28 players left in an event paying 27 places, the players will all play even tighter, in order to be sure they "make the money." This is the time to be sure you're stealing every blind you can steal! If no one is going to put up a fight, then make sure you grab all this "free money"! So what if you are eliminated in the "stink hole" (often called the "bubble")? In other words, so what if you finish twenty-eighth when the event is paying only 27 spots! Does twenty-seventh place change your life at all? If it does, then just do what everyone does and play supertight. Just be warned that I will be there picking up your blinds every round.

This strategy—"steal while they're in survival mode"—has helped me (and many other players) accumulate chips that become important when I'm later trying to advance into the final rounds and win the tournament. But you have to be a little careful with it. Enough players have learned about the strategy to defend the blinds with aggression of their own. Not everyone will go into a shell. You have to know your players and pick your spots.

SURVIVE AND THRIVE

Once you're in the money, things and people change. It's important that you take note of just what these changes are. If your opponents are playing too tight, steal their blinds. If they're playing too loose, you play a little bit tighter.

When you're in the money, you should still be waiting for some really high-quality hands before you get too involved in any pot. Remember that the limits are high, and you should be thinking about playing very tight, because at high limits losing one big pot can be devastating. If you can get away with stealing some blinds, do it; but with the limits way up there, every hand will cause a major swing in your chip count. So it's better just to sit back and watch the action and continue to survive. And when you do pick up a top ten hand, you'll be taking your shot at the pot with some power.

Sometimes I just wait for a big hand in a limit Hold'em tourney and let the cards decide how long I'll be around for that day. If I catch good cards and win, then I might win the whole enchilada. If I catch good cards and lose, then at least I'm happy that I went out with some top ten hands. If I don't catch anything decent and ante myself out of the tourney, that's OK too. But if I start playing hands that I'm not supposed to play, that's the worst of all, because I shoot myself in the foot!

BRING YOUR BIG GUNS TO A WAR!

When you have a border skirmish with someone, you don't need to bring out the heavy artillery, but when a war breaks out, you'd better bring your big guns! The same thing can be said about playing pots late in a poker tournament. You really don't need to have too much in your hand in order to try to steal the blinds from a mouse (a very cautious player). You probably won't need too much to defend your blinds against a jackal (a wildly aggressive player) either.

But when you decide to play a huge pot, then you'd better have a huge hand. I'm always looking for A-A, K-K, Q-Q, J-J, 10-10, or A-K before I get involved in a big pot. In fact, I never feel too bad after I've been eliminated late in a limit Hold'em event if I know that I lost some big pots with some big hands. Even though I hate losing a big pot late in one of these events with A-A, what more could I have asked than the chance to play a big pot with A-A? Ultimately, I feel pretty good knowing that an opponent had to put a lot of money into the pot with his Q-K or whatever against my A-A.

HOW TO TRAP WITH A BIG HAND

I've already told two stories (John Bonetti is featured trapping Dan Harrington in one story, on page 165) about how one player trapped another with A-A in the hole. In both stories, the player who was doing the trapping came out smelling like a rose. But trapping with pocket aces or pocket kings (especially kings, because they're vulnerable to a lone ace falling on the flop) can be extremely dangerous. By "trapping" with these hands, I mean just calling one or two bets before the flop, rather than raising or reraising with your hand. By just calling preflop and trapping other players into playing their hands when they ordinarily wouldn't have done this, you're creating a bigger pot, which means you're also risking losing a big pot.

For example, suppose that someone in front of you has raised with Q-Q, and then you decide to just call (smooth-call) with your K-K before the flop. Now someone with As-Js decides to call two bets with his hand, and then the board comes off 2s-4s-9h-3h-Ad. In this case, you would have won a huge pot from the opponent who had Q-Q if you had three-bet with your hand instead of calling two bets before the flop, because the As-Js would have folded before the flop and not hung around in hopes of catching a spade draw on the flop and the (for you) dreaded ace on the river. Imagine the number of bets that you would have won from the Q-Q in this scenario.

But because you decided to trap other players into the pot before the flop, you lost a big pot. Because the As-Js flopped the nut flush draw, he was forced to play his hand all the way, and then he hit an ace on the end to beat you.

Despite the grim scenario that I've just presented, trapping has its place in tournament poker, lest you become too predictable. But even I can't tell you exactly where that place is. One good time to trap is when you're in late position and no one else has entered the pot yet. This is a good place to just call one bet, to see if anyone else enters the pot behind you. In this scenario, if you make it two bets to go, then you'll probably just win the blinds. But by smooth-calling, you will at a minimum force the big blind to take a free flop. Just remember that in this case you're asking for action when you have a big hand. We all know that you should be very careful what you ask for, because you may get it!

Another time when I may smooth-call with A-A

or K-K is when I'm in the big blind and someone else has raised, and it's just myself and one other opponent in the pot. I smooth-call in order to trick my opponent into thinking I'm weak (that is, merely defending my mediocre blind hand), so that he will give me a lot of action the rest of the hand. Just remember that smooth-calling in limit Hold'em with big hands can work out very badly or perfectly, depending on the way the cards fall. When you smooth-call with a big hand, you really are gambling.

PLAY SATELLITES IN ORDER TO IMPROVE YOUR HOLD'EM GAME

If you want to win poker tournaments and not merely be satisfied with appearances at the final table, I strongly suggest that you play in satellites so that you become used to "endgame" poker play, that is, when the table is shorthanded with big stacks and big blinds. Satellites are ten-hand-ed minitournaments where players put up one-tenth of the buy-in to a poker tournament and the last player standing (actually, the last person sit-ting!) wins a seat in the main event.

For example, to play a satellite for the WSOP's first $2,000 buy-in limit Hold'em event (where several hundred players are expected each year), ten people put up $220 each, and the winner gets a seat in the $2,000 buy-in event. The seat allows the satellite winner to contend in an event that will pay more than $400,000 for first place! In this two-step process, you can run $220 into over $400,000 in two days!

Playing satellites simulates what it's like at the final table of a poker tournament. In order to win a satellite, you start out playing ten- or nine-handed and continue eliminating players until you're playing two-handed (heads-up) for the seat in the tournament.

Playing in multiple satellites also improves your shorthanded limit Hold'em nontournament game (in the side games). When you play nontourney Hold'em, you'll often find that the game will either end up shorthanded (five players or less) or become shorthanded for a time while you're waiting for new players to join up. If you have no experience in these shorthanded game situations, either you'll have to leave a potentially profitable game (when it fills up again) or you'll probably lose money, because shorthanded play is quite different from nine-handed play. Satellites let you practice and improve your shorthanded game, because you skip all the effort of getting to the "final table." You're already there, and as players start getting knocked out, you'll begin gaining experience that will help improve your shorthanded game.

PSYCHOLOGICAL ADVANTAGES IN POKER TOURNAMENTS

Making sure you're consistently friendly to the other players at the table is a wise policy. If players feel that you're a "good guy" or a friend, you increase the chance (at least marginally) that they won't call you in marginal situations where they could really hurt you, situations where they might well call someone they would love to bust.

Be careful with the great players at the table. I'm not saying that you should roll over and play dead; I'm just saying that it's probably not a good idea to steal their blinds, because they'll notice that. Remember that great players usually just want to last, so if you give them respect, they'll probably give you respect. If you start to "mess with them," though, they will mess with you, because they can. Believe me, you really don't want the great players messing with you! Try to be nice to everyone (really, I do try), and make sure that you give the great players respect. Only by giving respect will you get respect.

Limit Hold'em Tournaments: Summation

When you come to a limit Hold'em tournament, be prepared to sit down and play "top ten hands only" for the first five or six hours. If you're still in action five or six hours later, it's time to make sure that you are taking advantage of the mouse players at your table by stealing their blinds when you're in late position.

At this point in the tournament, you should still be trying to survive. You don't want to play a huge pot with a weak hand; save this sort of fancy playing until you are much farther along the experience curve. Rather, you want to play huge pots with top ten hands only.

If the players at your table are too loose, then play tight and just try to survive. If you happen to pick up a few cards (and to win a limit Hold'em tournament, you are going to have to pick up a few cards), you may win a couple of big pots from the loose players at the table. If the players at your table are too tight, then make sure that you're stealing a few blinds. If you're fortunate enough to make the final table, then draw on the experience you have gained playing all those satellites and focus on working your way into the final three spots, where most of the money is. Good luck to you when you play in a limit Hold'em tournament. Make sure that you learn something, and have a good time!

Eight

POKER ON THE INTERNET AND CYBER HOLD'EM STRATEGY

For centuries, poker had pretty much exactly the same form. Sure, there were subtle changes in rules and even in the card rooms where the game is played. But overall it remained fairly unchanged—that is, until the last year of the twentieth century. Then, just as with the rest of the business world, the Internet created enormous changes for poker.

Now you can learn about poker, read about poker, chat with people about poker, and, yes, even play poker anytime, from the comfort of your own home. The Internet has created an entirely new market for poker information and activities, and it is helping to create the fastest expansion in new players that we've ever seen.

People who were intimidated by formal poker rooms in the past now can learn the basics and risk very little money to play, with no loss of face when they make a dumb call or simply make an error. They can learn the game at their own pace, and risk virtually nothing to get some experience under their belt. (The economics of Internet games has made it possible to spread games that are much smaller than can be profitably spread in a casino, as small as a dime or quarter or even free!) And they have a chance to play and chat with people all over the world.

JUMPING ON THE WAVE

In 1998 I felt that I should have a website to generate some poker traffic—especially since I was living in the middle of Web hysteria in Silicon Valley, a place where you simply tried to generate traffic and then tried to figure out how to make money. In fact, if your website had enough hits, it was almost guaranteed to be worth some money, especially in the growing and lucrative gaming market.

The name was the easy part to decide on, and so philhellmuth.com was born. Inevitably, though, I had to decide on some goals and content for my site. Eventually I came up with two "reports" that I would post on philhellmuth.com; I called them "Hand of the Week" (HOW) and "High Limit Results" (HLR).

HOW would talk about some of the great poker pots that I have played, or witnessed, including key pots in each year's world championships and other major events. I pitched HOW to *Card Player* magazine (the industry's leading publication), and the editors loved it. I would write the HOW articles for the magazine and then archive them on my website. This launched my writing career, and the overwhelmingly positive feedback I received from readers made me think that I might have something worth offering.

The HLR articles are all written specifically for my site. They provide some insight into the biggest poker games in the world today. In HLR I write about the games played by high-limit poker players, and the $50,000-plus swings that we take in just a couple of hours! I write about the game we were playing in, who was in it, and where it was held. If you're interested, just go to philhellmuth.com and click on "Two Nines Room."

These days you can buy my books, my DVDs, my high-quality chip set, my "Poker Nights" ($50,000 a night personal appearances), Oakley sunglasses, and much more. We also have a

"Where's Phil?" section and a "What's Phil Up To?" section that gives details about my reality show ("Poker Protégé") and the movie project (*The Madison Kid*, which might be retitled *Poker Brat*).

PHILHELLMUTH.COM "LIVE" AND ARCHIVED AUDIO BROADCASTS

In an effort to drive traffic to philhellmuth.com, I dreamed of offering millions of people the chance to listen to the final table of the World Series of Poker (WSOP), the poker world's equivalent of a world championship, during a live Internet audio broadcast. A businessman friend of mine named Jeff Pulver (pulver.com) set up the site, and the first live audio broadcast of WSOP in 1999. We did it by "making it up as we went along," handing Andy Glazer's old clunker of a cell phone back and forth to different players for analysis.

In 1999, we had only 1,000 hits, but in 2000 we had tens of thousands of hits for our second WSOP broadcast. Then, as people became aware that we were doing the broadcasts, the number of hits started spiking up each year thereafter. The broadcasts from 1999, 2000, and 2001 are archived at my site and at UltimateBet.com (UB), though I have to admit that I have never listened to the broadcast from the year 2001, as it was by far the most disappointing poker day of my life! In 2001, I finished in fifth place in WSOP, which was worth $305,000; but first place had been worth $1.5 million and—more importantly to me—a lot of history.

THE NEXT STEP: ULTIMATEBET.COM (UB)

Now that I had a nice-looking website up and running (philhellmuth.com), I felt I should look into some other Web-related projects. A good friend of mine named David ("Porkchop") Wight had stopped playing poker professionally in order to run a business called Show Gear Productions. One day David told me that if I wanted to make money, I was in the wrong business—the Internet was the place to be. Finding a steady source of income sounded pretty good to me, since I knew that I could potentially lose all my money on any given day. The swings can drive a person toward insanity! As the old pros say, "Poker is a tough way to make an easy living."

David and I decided to look into starting an online poker room together, but after a few months he chose to devote all his time to his already thriving business, and I ended up consulting and promoting for UltimateBet.com, a beautiful online poker room which I believe in 100 percent and am fully committed to. I helped the software team that built UB with the poker rules, and I was also able to have some input in the concept side of the project.

For instance, the team implemented my idea of having five-handed tables available at the site. These "shorthanded" tables allow you to play a lot more pots, because the hand values are lower, so I recommend them to anyone who tends to be impatient or likes to be involved in a lot of pots.

In 2004, Summus and I had a cell phone Hold'em game that is cutting edge! Summus is a company in North Carolina that also has deals with the *Sports Illustrated* swimsuit edition for downloads and the *Wall Street Journal* for timely market information. "Phil Hellmuth's Texas Hold'em" game is available on most networks worldwide, and now you can play Hold'em anywhere at any time! Whether online or on a cell phone, the face of poker has changed overnight.

The bottom line for online poker: you can play from the comfort of your home, office, or hotel room and get in more than twice as many hands per hour. At UB, you can even play free. And while it's not the same as playing face-to-face, sometimes

I like it even better! I recommend that you give online poker a try before you spend any serious time in a "brick-and-mortar" card room. You can often find me playing small-stakes online poker at UB. Look for the name "PhilHellmuth." But pay attention to some of my hints in this chapter, because you'll need to alter your strategy a little when you make the transition. In this chapter you will learn:

> ➢ Deception and reading in Cyber Hold'em.
> ➢ Ten-handed Cyber strategy.
> ➢ Five-handed Cyber strategy.
> ➢ Limit Hold'em two-handed (heads-up) theory.
> ➢ Limit Hold'em heads-up: Howard Lederer's theory.
> ➢ About rec.gambling.poker.com (RGP), the online "newsgroup" for poker.
> ➢ About UltimateBet.com, an online poker room.
> ➢ About philhellmuth.com, my website with my "Hand of the Week," live Internet broadcasts, pictures, and more.
> ➢ About CardPlayer.com, the information website for the industry-leading *Card Player* magazine, with tournament results and more.
> ➢ About PokerPages.com, the website with tons

of information about poker, tournaments, and much more.

ONLINE POKER STRATEGY

Now it is time to move on to the strategy part of this strategy chapter! First, I'll talk about playing ten-handed Texas Hold'em—by far the most popular game on the Internet (especially limit Hold'em). Second, I will cover the best strategy for five-handed games. Finally, I will talk about how to play two-handed (heads-up) Hold'em games. Most of the information that I dole out here will refer you back to certain sections that you have already read earlier in this book. For example, my section on full-game limit Hold'em for the Internet will refer you to Chapter 3 of this book and the "top ten only" strategy that I talk about there. The new information about strategy that you will read in this section will have to do with playing five-handed games and two-handed games.

If you would like online strategy for ten-handed Hold'em, I recommend that you simply follow my section on beginners' strategy. I would program a computer exactly like this so that it could take advantage of online players' primary weakness—

they play too many hands before the flop. In other words, they have no patience! One thing you can depend on: my sections for beginners all counsel plenty of patience. Now you just need to use these patience strategies to crush your online opponents in the small-stakes games!

LIMIT HOLD'EM ON THE INTERNET: DECEPTION AND READING

Limit Hold'em is a fast-moving game for a fast-moving society, and I have noticed that online players seem to move into and out of games more quickly. Online players are often playing on their lunch break at the office, or they just have an hour to kill before dinner or before going out at night. In any case, the lineups change quickly, and so you don't have a lot of time to figure out what the other players are doing. Therefore, you need to notice which players are doing what in order to determine what type of players they are. Pay particularly close attention to the hands that they show at the end of a pot. If a player has raised a pot and then bet all the way down to the end and shows 6d-7c, you know that he is a jackal type. (My animal types are discussed in Chapter 3, page 42.)

You'll be able to determine what kinds of players

your opponents are by the number of pots they play and the type of hands they show down. If you notice that a player hasn't played a pot in a while, the early evidence suggests that he may be a mouse type. Of course, if you play at the same online room over and over again, you will start to understand from past experience what types of players the others are.

Remember, though, that the sword cuts both ways in online poker. The other players won't know anything about you except what you let them see. If you are raising a lot of pots, the other players will think that you are a jackal, especially if you show down some weaker hands. You may show some of your weaker hands at the end of the hand even if you don't win the pot, in order to convey the illusion that you are a jackal. Or you can show your strong hands faceup at the end of a hand in order to give people the impression that you are a mouse. In general, I like to show my strong starting hands faceup, to make people think I am a mouse. Then I will be able to bluff more pots in the future, because they will think I always play a big hand. (In lower-limit games, however, it is pretty hard to bluff someone out on the end!) Even though you can't read other people's facial expressions, there is still plenty of information available about the way they play Hold'em. You can also confuse the other players by showing down weak or strong hands in order to give them the wrong impression about the way you play Hold'em.

Other things to watch include the amount of time a player takes to make a decision, and the number of other games a player is in. If players are in another game, they are likely to lose concentration, and you may be able to take advantage of this weakness by playing more aggressively against them. A good online "tell" is whether or not a player bets his hand right away. Sometimes you can figure out if a quick bet means a hand or a bluff. A quick bet is usually a sign of weakness, and a slow bet is usually a sign of strength. Everyone in poker is an actor, and when people bet slowly they are usually trying to say to you, "I don't know if I should bet this hand or not. Let me think. I'm pretty weak right now." At least that's what they want you to think when they bet slowly on the end. By contrast, a quick bet is meant to convey an impression of strength; they're saying, "I have a huge hand, and I'm going to bet because of this." You might not want to believe it, though!

LIMIT HOLD'EM STRATEGY: TEN-HANDED GAMES

I am recommending that you use the "top ten only" strategy when you play online poker at a ten-handed table. The strategy of the "top ten" hands is laid out in Chapter 3 of this book. This strategy is simple, safe, and very effective. Using this strategy should allow you to build up some profits while you play online poker. If I could design a computer program to play my money online, this is the way I would program it.

The reason I recommend this slow strategy is that the online players in small-stakes poker games play so badly that the "top ten" strategy will be a big winner in the long haul. There is no need to get fancy and take big swings up and down with your money online: the patient route will smooth out the swings and produce the desired wins. Make sure that you play in games of an appropriate size for your bankroll. If you intend to risk $100 online, make sure that you play no higher than $1–$2 limit. This way you will have 50 big bets to play with, and you will give the "top ten" strategy a chance to succeed for you. With 50 big bets, you will have a decent shot at turning $100 into a lot more money over 40 hours of play using my online strategy.

However, 50 big bets are still not much money in a poker game, and 100 big bets are a much safer amount to start with. Please do not be discouraged if you lose your initial $100 playing the "top ten" strategy. Luck is a big part of poker, and although this strategy is a favorite in any online $1–$2 game, sometimes you can just get unlucky!

LIMIT HOLD'EM STRATEGY: FIVE-HANDED GAMES

Hold'em is a very different game when you are playing it at a table where the maximum is five players. You will find that the swings you take in a five-handed game will tend to be much bigger than the swings you take at a ten-handed table. Beware of this and understand that it is just the nature of the beast! Five-hand-maximum tables don't exist right now in the "real world," probably because the casinos figure they have a limited amount of space and need to use it for full-size tables. Online casinos, of course, face no such limitation.

So this strategy can be used only online or any time that the online game you're playing in gets down to five hands. At a five-hand-maximum table, we can now add all small pairs, any A-x, and "20" (two cards that add up to 20 or more) to the mix of hands we can play before the flop. Of course, I'm not saying that you can play these additional hands all the time. For example, I wouldn't play 10-J for three bets before the flop. However, you can now call two bets with these types of hands or make it two bets yourself with them. Because you are playing more than three times as many hands before the flop in a five-handed game as in a ten-handed game, you may also find five-handed tables a lot more fun, and potentially a lot more profitable.

When you play five-handed poker it is more important to find out where you're at in a hand on the flop. I cover this concept very thoroughly in Chapter 3. Also, if you have a hand like A-K or A-Q you will end up calling your opponents down a lot more often when you don't hit your hand, so you will naturally be exposing yourself to more risk.

LIMIT HOLD'EM TWO-HANDED (HEADS-UP) THEORY

Heads-up poker is strategically much different from a full game. Interestingly, some players who are jackals in a full game tend to do very well in a heads-up game. Perhaps the reason is that they are already used to playing many hands aggressively. Being a tough player in a nine-handed Hold'em game requires patience, discipline, and aggressive play. However, being a tough player in a heads-up Hold'em game requires superaggressive play, good reads in almost every hand, and the ability to play bad hands well (so to speak). Notice that I didn't mention patience as an important trait in a tough heads-up player. This is because patient players usually don't learn how to play bad hands well.

Knowing when to bet with bottom pair on the end because you are certain that your opponent has ace high is an important ability in a heads-up match. In other words, knowing if and when you have the best hand is extremely important in heads-up play. While this may be important in any game of poker, you'll have to do it far more often in heads-up play.

When you're playing against a player who bluffs out against you all the time heads-up, I recommend that you smooth-call with a lot of hands on the flop and on fourth street, and then raise on the river.

Slow-Playing Against a Superaggressive Player

Often, you will find yourself playing heads-up with a superaggressive player. When this is the case, I like to slow-play my hands. Suppose that I have Q-Q in the pocket and the aggressive player has raised on the button. Most of the time in this situation, I will just call him before the flop to trap him later on. Suppose that the flop is J-8-5. Now I like to check and just call again! Give him a little rope. Let's say that the next card off is a deuce for J-8-5-2. Now I check again, and if my opponent bets, now I finally raise! If I trap my opponent here, he will be less likely to try to bluff on every hand, because he knows that I am capable of trapping him again soon!

Limit Hold'em Heads-Up: Howard Lederer's Theory

Limit Hold'em is a very different game heads-up. I know of one great player, Howard Lederer (Annie Duke's older brother), who will raise every time that he has the button in heads-up Hold'em, and it seems to work well for him! Raising every hand when you have the button is a really good strategy to use against a novice. The idea is to raise every hand on the button and then bet every flop. When you do this, you're giving your opponent a chance to fold his hand every time you make a bet. You're putting pressure on him constantly and forcing him to call you down with some really weak hands.

This is really hard for anyone to handle—especially since a high percentage of the time in Hold'em you don't even flop a pair! However, if you're up against a tough player, you're in trouble when you play like this. My counterstrategy for this is simply to reraise every time I have ace high, king high, two cards above a nine, or a pair. And then I bet out at them every flop!

MORE INFORMATION: REC.GAMBLING.POKER.COM IS THE ONLINE "NEWSGROUP" FOR POKER

If you are interested, an online poker newsgroup is located at rec.gambling.poker.com (RGP). RGP has a big voice in the poker world today, and the RGP group meets every year to play poker at the Big August Recreational Gambling Excursion (BARGE) in Las Vegas. I was the keynote speaker for BARGE in 2001, and I had a great time hanging out with the RGP regulars. Their enthusiasm for poker is very refreshing and contagious! Imagine poker games spontaneously breaking out on the floor of a room that RGP was renting or poker tournaments with teams of four players each!

Often, people will start threads involving poker strategy that are both illuminating and interesting to read, and it is always interesting to me how others think poker hands ought to be played. Other threads talk about the latest rumors concerning players and poker tournaments. (Everyone has a voice on RGP, and unfortunately some voices are a little bit too loud and negative, at least for my taste.) One particularly useful thing you can learn from RGP is where the local poker game in your area is played and what the stakes are. Just ask! By the way, you'll find that "newbies" are always welcome at RGP.

One thing I should point out if you are going to visit RGP: not everyone who offers advice really knows what he is talking about, although people try to make it sound as if they know a lot. Be cautious about taking advice on RGP as gospel, at least until you figure out who the more trustworthy posters are.

RESOURCES

Love it or hate it, the Internet has made an indelible mark on the poker landscape. More people are learning about poker and playing it because of the ease of access to learning tools and free or low-stakes games online. And there doesn't appear to be any turning back . . . the Internet is here to stay.

I don't think it's a coincidence that tournaments and card rooms around the world are seeing record attendance; people who learn online are eager to try what they learn face-to-face!

You can also bet that there will be more and more opportunities to get into profitable games online. The play tends to be loose and fast, and solid players with excellent fundamentals should be able to make the games pay off. The opportunities are even better when you factor in the chance to play at multiple tables at the same time, and to do so in your favorite easy chair!

With the Internet's ease of access and its ability to grow quickly, I think it's only a matter of time before we see 25,000 people in an online tournament. I don't know about you, but I'm likely to be one of them!

Here are some resources that you might find helpful.

To Practice and Play Online

ULTIMATEBET.COM: This is the only site that I currently recommend. It's regulated by the Kahnawake Gaming Commission and is honest and professional. I also happen to think that UB's game is the only one that will really let you concentrate. It's the only place that I'd play. Period.

Poker Articles and Information

PHILHELLMUTH.COM: See pages 232–235.

CARDPLAYER.COM: A great site that offers many of the same resources as the magazine, but in an electronic format. You can find many great articles written by some of the best poker writers in the business, including myself. There is also information about where and when upcoming poker tournaments are being held and results from past tournaments. Barry and Jeff Shulman have done a great job with this site and also with *Card Player* magazine.

POKERPAGES.COM: More information than you can believe on the game of poker. If it's out there, I can usually find it at PokerPages, including tournament results, schedules, online articles, links, and a sharp "Online Poker School." Tina and Mark Napolitano have done a wonderful job with this site, and they also managed to bring Mike "the Mad Genius" Caro on to help.

LAST NOTES ON PLAYING ONLINE

The legal landscape surrounding the online gaming industry is constantly shifting and being revised as lawmakers wrestle with some of the legal challenges that online gaming poses. While many of the legal issues seem to be undecided, you should check your local laws before playing poker online for money. It may not be allowed in your area.

Nine

HOW TO WIN A NO-LIMIT HOLD'EM TOURNAMENT

Am I committing professional suicide by writing this chapter? Will Erik Seidel be sore at me? Suicide, no; Seidel, yes. Erik is notorious for not wanting to give away information, but he should bear in mind that whatever else you do, you still have to read people well if you're going to win a no-limit Hold'em tournament—and not just reach the money.

I'll be giving you a decent blueprint in this brief chapter, but you will still need to decide when (precisely) you should make your moves. The top pros will know this stuff, but most other players won't, and even one good tip can make the difference between winning and losing.

I wouldn't have written this chapter except for the fact that I included this world-class strategy in my new DVD (*Phil Hellmuth's Million Dollar Tournament Strategies*). In that DVD session, I just kept on talking, and they just kept on filming, and before long I knew I'd given away too many secrets. All the same, I felt I had made the best tournament strategy DVD yet produced. And since I gave away too much there, I thought it only right that I give away too much here!

In formulating the strategy that I recommend in this chapter, I have in mind the World Series of Poker's $2,000 buy-in no-limit Hold'em, or other big NLH events like it. You will have to adjust your play for smaller buy-in (less than $1,600) events, which are usually structured for a faster pace, and you'll really need to adjust for Internet tournaments like the UltimateBet.com ones, which ramp up very quickly. Nonetheless, this strategy is universal and should serve you well for all NLH events.

In this chapter, you will be learning how to play:

- ➢ The beginning stages: steal the blinds? No!
- ➢ The early ante stages: take control?
- ➢ Playing a short stack and a big stack.
- ➢ Later on, well after the dinner break.
- ➢ Steal just before you hit the money positions.

➤ The dynamics of the final 18.

➤ Your choices at the final table.

➤ The final three, a different game: reads, baby!

➤ The endgame: practice, practice, practice.

THE BEGINNING STAGES: STEAL THE BLINDS? NO!

With the blinds low relative to stack size, and no antes required yet, it is important to stick to a "top ten" only strategy—especially when the pot has been raised before the flop. But with this stricture in mind as a starting point, we need to open the door a bit to other hands in unraised pots. This can be a good time to play hands like A-x suited, suited connectors like 8h-7h, and small pairs. Again, I say: in unraised pots. The attraction is that you may win a lot of money if you hit these kinds of hands occasionally.

The reason to play supertight when there is no ante, and when no one has raised before the flop, is that you can steal only small amounts of money even when you do raise the pot. Say the blinds are $100–$200, and everyone has $5,000 in chips. Every time you pop it up to, say, $600 to go, in order to steal the blinds, you're making $300 profit ($100 + $200). Which means you're risking $600 to make $300 each blind-stealing raise.

But when the blinds are $100–$200 with a $25 a player ante (as required in later rounds of most tournaments), then you win $525 at a nine-handed table ($100 + $200 + $225). In this case, you risk $600 to win $525, which is a much better yield. If the blind steal works 50 percent of the time, then you are losing a little bit of money, but if it works 75 percent of the time (75 percent is the traditional average), then you're doing really well. Of course, if you wait for one player to call in front of you before you raise it up, then you would win $725 a pop, which means that you're making money even if everyone folds only 50 percent of the time.

So it makes sense to sit back and wait for the antes to kick in before you get too involved with blind stealing, or with moving over the top of the other blind stealers. Of course, once the antes are in effect, you know that more people are attempting to steal the blinds, and this is another reason to come over the top of people later, rather than sooner.

So sit back, play patiently for the first few pre-ante levels, in hopes that you will have a couple of nice situations come up and propel you to some kind of profit. But be sure to pay attention to the others at your table in order to gain insight into their play. Do they check-raise when they hit a big hand, or do they bet it? Try to sharpen up your reads on the opponents at your table. These reads will allow you either to make good moves on your opponents later, or to make good lay downs against them.

Remember that "the game is on" only after you hit the antes, and patience will help you make it that far.

THE EARLY ANTE STAGES: TAKE CONTROL?

At this point in the tournament there is a better mathematical argument for "getting involved" (making blind steals or coming over the top of others who are presumably making blind steals). But certain players (me, on occasion) like to sit back and let others "do the dirty work." These players like to let the other players go crazy, and then nail them when they finally do have a nice hand. It just depends on who is at your table, and what they seem to be doing.

A lot of times I will sit back and let other players outplay me for long periods of time, and then "felt them" (bust them, leaving nothing but felt). I let them think they can outplay me, even going so far as folding the best hand more than once when the hand is close, which encourages them to feel comfortable moving in on me; then bang, they're busted. Many times these days I'm forced to sit back and set the bait, but I will always take what the table gives me, and I'll raise and reraise when I have good reads (or good hands), or when the table is particularly passive.

So at an aggressive table, I will relax and wait until the aggressive players give me their chips (or outdraw me!). And when I'm at a passive table, I will control the action by making raises and reraises.

PLAYING A SHORT STACK AND A BIG STACK

An axiom that I love states basically that when you have little money, then take tons of chances, but when you have a ton of money, quit taking chances altogether. In my life I have found that this axiom manifests itself naturally: when I started winning big poker tournaments, I gave up riding motorcycles and piloting small planes. Why take chances now that I had a future?

In poker tournaments the same thing has generally been true for me. When I have a ton of chips, then there is no need for me to gamble and take chances by playing weak hands. Status quo is good, protecting chips is better, and having a winning situation come up when I have a big stack—because I waited for it—is the best! So remember to protect your chips when you're in the lead in a tournament.

On the other hand, when you have no chips, and not too much to lose, then you can take a few chances. I'm not saying that you should go crazy, just that you should make a few more all-in moves. For example, with $2,000 left and the blinds at $200–$400 with a $50 ante, you should be thinking, "I need that $1,050 in ante and blind money!" If I have, say, Q-9 two positions off of the button with no callers, I like moving all-in here better than folding. If I win the pot uncontested, then I move up in chips at least 50 percent, from $2,000 to $3,050. A few well-timed moves like that and your chip position changes quickly.

Some champions like to use their big stacks to bully everyone else, but that tactic seems to work less and less lately, since the new players have figured out, for whatever reason (TV!), what we're doing. They no longer just fold their A-J off suit when they should (or at least when *we* think they should), instead choosing to make a stand with it.

LATER ON, WELL AFTER
THE DINNER BREAK

If you're still in there late with at least average chip stacks, then whatever you're doing that day is working. Don't change it until you reach the final 12 players or so. Stick to what brought you there for the next few levels of play. Pay attention to some of the older players or the more fatigued players, because many of them will become easier to read the later the hour. When players get tired, they will make more mistakes, and will lean too heavily on the very character that makes up their nature.

Some will be fighting all day long to play tight enough, and then suddenly revert to their more natural loose style. Some will be avoiding the over-the-top move that they love, but now they lose their discipline and start coming over the top. Some will simply disintegrate under the pressure—more often than not, that happens somewhere among the final 18 players.

STEAL JUST BEFORE YOU HIT
THE MONEY POSITIONS

In the 2003 WSOP's $3,000 buy-in no-limit

Hold'em event, with 28 players left and 27 getting paid, I tried a little experiment. With the blinds at $1,000–$2,000, and the antes at $300 a player, I made it $5,000 to go without looking at my cards. Everyone folded, and I piled the $5,100 ($1,000 SB + $2,000 BB + $2,100 antes [7 x $300] = $5,100) into my $80,000 stack. My theory here was that I thought that everyone wanted to be sure to make the money, and would thus fold rather than risk finishing in the "stink hole" as it is called on tour.

So I popped it up the next hand too — without looking at my cards — making it $5,000 to go; and when everyone folded, I had picked up $10,200 without ever looking at my cards! Right then I decided I would raise every pot until someone played back at me, or I lost a pot. On the fourth hand, someone finally called me, but fortunately my "blind hand" was pocket aces, and I won that pot too!

I raise, they fold, and so it went until the thirteenth hand, when I raised it up from the first position, and someone finally called me from the big blind. It turned out that I had the 6c-5c, and the flop was A-2-3. After stealing $60,000 in pots, I decided to check and give up the pot — of course I was hoping for a four to make a straight.

When a six came off of the deck, my opponent, WSOP legend Billy Baxter, bet out $8,000 into the $12,000 pot. I wasn't sure that he had anything at this point, so I called him with my pair of sixes. The last card was a four, which made me a straight, A-2-3-4-5! Now he checked, and I bet out $17,000, and he folded quickly. (I think he was bluffing and couldn't beat my pair of sixes, never mind my straight.)

Since the strategy was now working so well, I kept on raising it up, and they kept on folding. The players at the table would say, "I folded A-J that hand." I would say, "I'm really hitting some great hands today!" Quite a number of spectators were in the stands close by watching, and I heard a few comments like, "Phil has 9-4 off suit" or "Phil had 6-2 off suit." Of course, I didn't know what I had most of those hands, but I'm sure the spectators were about right!

Finally, on hand number 23, I was in the small blind, and someone (Doc Barry) raised it up in early position. There I sat with Q-J off suit, not wanting the run to end quite yet. After all, while winning 22 pots in a row I had stolen $110,000 in chips, and picked up more when my A-A beat Doc Barry and my 6c-5c beat Billy Baxter. But I finally decided just to fold the Q-J, and be happy with what had transpired the last 22 hands. I now had over $200,000 in chips, and only one other player was even close. Erik Seidel had about $110,000 and was doing the same thing I was doing, I'm sure!

Anyway, the moral of the story is this: if the other players at your table are playing for 27th place, then let them have 27th place! No one at my table wanted to finish 28th that day, and thus they kept folding their hands, while waiting for someone else to go broke. I'm in WSOP tournaments to win, and if everyone is going to fold like a house of cards, then I'll scoop up all those precious chips and use them to my advantage later on.

There weren't a lot of smiles at my table after that run, but one thing is certain: everyone at my table got what they wanted; they all made the final 27 players (and the prize money)! By the way, I got what I wanted too: I went on to win my record-tying ninth WSOP bracelet the next day (and $420,000).

THE DYNAMICS OF THE FINAL 18

Things change as people smell the big money and the big prize. Disintegration, fatigue, and loss of effective play all hit about now. It's like watching the final holes of one of the four golf majors: the pressure is on and the choking begins for many players. But on day one, many times, the goal is simply to make day two. If that was your goal, then keep this in mind.

Sometimes, players are so desperate to make day two that they fold an absurd number of hands, and you can make a good number of blind steals to fortify your stack for the final table battle the next day, and the big money. (Remember that the big money goes to only the final three spots in most poker tournaments.)

So you do have to pay attention to making the final table, but be sure to watch for opportunities to steal some extra blinds along the way, as the table goes from 18 players down to 10. If you do go out, then fine. Just make sure that you have a good "bad beat" story. Don't disintegrate!

YOUR CHOICES AT THE FINAL TABLE

Again, the big money is usually in the top three spots. So it is time to go one way or the other. Try either to make the top three with whatever the universe provides while playing patiently, or go for it and try to accumulate a ton of chips stealing blinds while the other players try to move up a few spots. Most times I'll sit back patiently and "pick off" the go-for-it type of players. I think I'm able to do this largely because almost everyone else seems to go crazy or disintegrate.

But if everyone else is sitting back way too often, then I'll go for it, and in general pick up a lot of chips virtually risk-free. It is a fine line to walk, and if I decide to go for it, then reading the other players perfectly becomes essential. One bad read and I'm crippled or gone!

Generally, when you reach the final three, a deal is made that involves some sort of redistribution of the money. For example, with the prizes set at $400,000 for first, $200,000 for second, and $100,000 for third a few years back, I turned down a deal when I had the chip lead. The deal would have locked up $250,000 for me at Harrah's championship event in 1999. Whoops! I finished third after two bad beats (my Ad-Qd all-in vs. his Ah-6s for a $400,000 pot, followed closely by his K-J vs. my A-10 for over $400,000), and left the table steaming out of my mind from these beats (although for once I handled myself admirably), and pissed off with "merely" $100,000. By the way, the WPT has outlawed all future deals—perhaps because they want to see us players under extreme pressure!

Of course, in a few other situations like that I

chose not to make a deal, and it panned out well. On one of those occasions, I left with all of the first-place money and the coveted WSOP bracelet, my ninth! (See my new book *Bad Beats and Lucky Draws*, under "Bracelet Number Nine," with Erik Seidel and Daniel Negreanu at the 2003 WSOP.)

THE FINAL THREE, A DIFFERENT GAME: READS, BABY!

The only way to get better at playing the final three is through practice. Hold'em becomes a totally different game three-handed, and much more read-dependent. If you expect or hope to win a no-limit Hold'em tournament, then you better work on your shorthanded game. It's important to understand the changing dynamics of shorthanded Hold'em, and to get accustomed to playing this way.

THE ENDGAME: PRACTICE, PRACTICE, PRACTICE

These days you can improve your final-table proficiency and shorthanded play by playing one-table satellites—with ten players—online at places like UltimateBet.com (called a "sit-and-go").

Another nice learning tool now available to most of us is cell phone Hold'em. It's amazing to me to see the graphics handled so well on such a small interface! Of course I prefer "Phil Hellmuth's Texas Hold'em" game to the other cell phone games.

Now that you have a valuable overview (I charge $25,000 a night for lessons!) of the correct way to play no-limit Hold'em tournaments—stage by stage—I'll see you soon on the World Poker Tour or at the World Series of Poker!

Appendix

Rank of Hands in Poker

The best possible hand in poker (Hold'em is a poker game!) is the royal flush. I have made only two in my career so far! Here is the rank of hands, in order from strongest to weakest. There are four suits in poker—clubs, diamonds, hearts, and spades.

1. Royal flush (10s-Js-Qs-Ks-As)—the ten through the ace, all of the same suit.
2. Straight flush—five cards in a row (straight), all in the same suit. A royal flush is simply an ace-high straight flush. The 2c-3c-4c-5c-6c (six-high straight flush) and 7d-8d-9d-10d-Jd (jack-high straight flush) are straight flushes.
3. Four of a kind (quads)—having all four of a card number, like 6c-6d-6h-6s (four sixes) or 8c-8d-8h-8s (four eights), qualifies as four of a kind.

4. Full house (full boat or boat)—three of a kind and two of a kind in one hand. For example, 5d-5h-5s-Kd-Ks (fives full of kings) or Js-Jh-Jd-2s-2d (jacks full of twos) or 9d-9c-9h-7d-7s (nines full of sevens).

5. Flush—having all five of your cards in one suit qualifies as a flush. For example, 2s-5s-7s-Js-Ks (king-high flush) or 5h-7h-Jh-Qh-Ah (ace-high flush) or any combination of five to a suit makes a flush.

6. Straight—five cards in a row in number order, but not all in the same suit. Two examples are 3d-4s-5h-6h-7c (seven-high straight) and 9h-10s-Jh-Qs-Kc (king-high straight).

7. Three of a kind (trips or a set)—having three of a card number, such as 4s-4d-4h (trip fours or "set of fours") or Jh-Js-Jd (trip jacks or "set of jacks").

8. Two pair—two of a kind twice in one hand. Examples are Ah-Ac-4d-4h-9h (aces up) or Js-Jh-2c-2s-7h (jacks up) and 7h-7d-3h-3s-Ac (sevens up).

9. One pair—two of a kind. Examples are As-Ac-9h-6h-3s (aces) and 8h-8s-Js-2c-4h (eights).

10. High cards—highest five cards from the top down. Examples are As-Qd-6h-4s-2c (ace-queen high), As-Jc-6d-5h-3s (ace-jack high),

and Ks-Jd-8d-6h-3c (king-jack high). A-Q
beats A-9 high, and A-Q-J-9 beats A-Q-J-8
high.

Don't be put off by these seemingly complicated
rankings! Most big poker pots are won by one pair
or two pair or three of a kind (trips). This ranking
stuff comes very easily once you begin to play
poker. And the rankings above match those in the
family game around the kitchen table.

Phil's Glossary

A-x suited—Having for hole cards an ace and an undercard of the same suit, like Ad-5d or As-Js.

Action—Gambling or loose betting: "The action was tremendous." "I want some of that action." "Give me some of that action."

Advertising—Making a loose play with the intent of looking like a loose player, thus inducing extra action from your opponents in later hands.

All-in—When you move all of your chips remaining into the pot: "Jeff just moved all-in for $95,000!" If you lose the pot, you're out of the tournament.

All-in protection—The "anti-billionaire" rule, the concept that you cannot be "bet out of," or be eliminated from, a pot just because you run out of money on the table. For example, if the pot holds $165 and you have only $79 left, you may call that portion of your opponent's $200 bet by putting all $79 of your chips in the pot. If you win the pot, you can win the whole $165 main pot and $79 of his $200.

American Airlines—Pocket aces, A-A.

Ante—In some poker games, the amount of money or chips that each player puts into the pot before the cards are dealt.

Backdoor—Catching two cards in a row to make a particular hand. "I made the backdoor flush and won a huge pot."

Bad beat—An unlucky, often unlikely, turn of events that causes you to lose a hand. "Ouch, that was a really bad beat!"

Banker—The player at a table who is responsible for passing out the chips and keeping track of the money and credit.

Bankroll (BR)—The amount of money you have that you will risk on poker or any other endeavor. "Right now he has a $2,500 bankroll to work with."

Belly buster—See "Inside straight draw."

Bet—Initiate the betting after a new card is dealt. When no one has bet in front of you and it is your turn to act, you may bet or check or fold.

Betting out, betting into—See "Bet."

Betting round—Betting that occurs from the time a new card is dealt until the action set in motion by that card is complete. "I won the pot on the last betting round with a bluff!"

Bettor—The player who first voluntarily puts money

into the pot in a given betting round (thus the blinds are not seen as bettors).

Big blind—The blind who sits two to the left of the button. The big blind usually costs that player one betting unit. See also "Blinds" and "Small blind." "I folded in the big blind, but I would have won a big pot."

Big money streets—In limit poker, the betting rounds in which the bets are doubled. For example, in a $10- to $20-limit game the big money streets are the rounds when you bet $20.

Blank—A card that doesn't help your hand. "There were a ton of cards that would have made my hand, so I was disappointed to see two blanks."

Blinds—The money posted by the two players directly to the left of the button, before the cards are dealt, and the designation of the players posting it. There are two blinds, and the amount posted by the small blind is generally half the size of that posted by the big blind.

Bluff—A bet that conveys to others that you have a stronger hand than you actually have.

Board—The faceup community cards placed in the middle by the dealer in Hold'em.

Boat—A full house. Sometimes referred to as a "full boat."

Broadway—An ace-high straight (10-J-Q-K-A).

Broke—See "Busted."

Bubble—The highest nonpaying spot in a poker tournament. For example, nineteenth place in a tournament that pays the final eighteen players.

Building a pot—Raising or reraising in order to increase the amount of money in the pot.

Busted—Out of money; out of chips in a poker tournament. "Poor Big Al, he's busted again." "I just busted out of the tournament."

Button—The physical and symbolic designation of the person who is "dealing," whether actually dealing or not, and therefore last to act in the betting rounds of that hand.

Buy another card—Call a bet to see the next card dealt.

Buy-in—The amount of money you start playing with in a game, or the prescribed amount it costs to enter a poker tournament.

Call—Match another player's bet. When someone bets, you may fold, call, or raise. See also "Reraise."

Calling (someone) down—Calling all of another player's bets, because you believe that you have a better hand.

Calling station—Someone who calls other players too often.

Capped—Said of a pot holding the maximum number of bets allowed in a limit poker game on any given betting round. A capped pot in Las Vegas holds five bets; a capped pot in Los Angeles holds four bets.

Cashed—Placed in the money (the paying spots) at the conclusion of a poker tournament.

Catching a card—Having a card come that was one of the cards needed to win a pot. For example, the instance where someone needs a flush card and it comes. "I caught the perfect card on the last card."

Chasing—Trying continually to hit long shots.

Check—Choose not to bet, but to stay in the hand. When no one has bet yet, you too have the option not to bet, without folding your hand.

Check-raise—Check and then raise within one betting round. You may check initially when no one else has bet yet and then, when it is your turn to act again, raise someone else's bet.

Chip and a chair—The circumstance when someone has only a couple of chips or a single chip left in a tournament.

Cold—When the game seems to be going poorly and you've been winning few pots over a period of at least an hour. "John sure was cold at the end of that tournament."

Cold call—Call three or four bets without having invested any money previously in the pot. "Can you believe that he called three bets cold with that garbage?"

Community card—Faceup card that may be used by any player at the table to strengthen or complete a hand.

Cowboys—A pair of kings, K-K.

Dead—See "Drawing dead."

Dealer's choice—A variety of poker in which the dealer has the option of choosing the game.

Dealing—Giving out the cards to the players and the board, throughout an entire hand.

Declare—State whether you are pursuing a high or a low hand.

Double up—Increase your chip stack 100 percent.

Down cards—A player's private hole cards, which are dealt facedown and which only he can see. See also "Facedown" and "Hole cards."

Draw—A situation in which a player needs a particular card to complete a poker hand; for example, a seven for a 5-6-8-9 inside straight draw.

Drawing dead—When a player cannot win the hand, regardless of what cards come up. "I had him drawing dead that hand."

Drawing hand—See "Draw."

Dry aces—A pair of aces with no other draws.

Ducks—Pocket deuces, 2-2 hole cards.

Dump—Fold.

Eagle—A world-class poker player. One of the "animal personalities" that I use to teach you strategy.

Early position—One of the three table positions to the immediate left of the big blind.

Elephant—A player who plays too many hands and calls too many bets. One of the "animal personalities" that I use to teach you poker strategy.

Endgame—A strategy employed when there are five or fewer players left in a poker tournament.

Even-money pot—A situation in which a player's chance of winning the pot is roughly 50 percent.

Facedown—Placed (as a hole card) with its face down, so that only its owner can take a look at it.

Faceup—Placed (as a community card) with its face up, so that all players can see it throughout the hand.

Family poker game (home-style poker)—The kind of poker game that you might play with your close friends, coworkers, or family, usually involving low stakes and wild cards.

Fast—Loose and aggressive style that includes lots of betting and raising, and involves a lot of hands. "He's the fastest player in the game."

Fifth street—In Hold'em, the dealing of the fifth and final community card and the ensuing round of betting. Also called "the river." "Amarillo Slim is so darn lucky that he catches whatever he needs on fifth street."

Final table—The final nine players remaining in a Hold'em tournament.

Flat call—An instance in which a player with a powerful hand calls instead of raising, in hopes of encouraging action.

Flop—The first three community cards dealt in Hold'em, all faceup on the board. All three are flipped up at once, and as community cards all players can use them. "That was a beautiful flop for my hand."

Flopping—Making a hand on the flop. "I flopped the straight and won a huge pot."

Flush—A hand consisting of any five cards of the same suit, such as 5s-7s-8s-Js-Ks.

Flush draw—A situation in which a player has four cards of the same suit, thus needing only one more of that suit to make a flush hand.

Folding—Conceding the pot either by throwing your hole cards away or by a verbal declaration ("I fold").

Four of a kind—A hand consisting of four cards of the same rank, such as 6c-6s-6h-6d.

Fourth street—In Hold'em, the dealing of the fourth community card and the ensuing round of betting. Also called "the turn." "On fourth street, the five of diamonds came off and I made a flush."

Free card—A situation in which no bets are made on a given round of betting.

Free roll—A situation in which you are sure to win but also have an opportunity to coax further amounts into the pot.

Full ring play—In a side (nontournament) game, playing with the maximum number of players allowed, usually nine.

Game theory—Tactics and strategy for a particular game, poker or otherwise; the analysis of a situation involving conflicting interests.

Garbage—A weak hand. "Why do you always play that garbage?"

Good shape—A situation in which a player has a high probability of winning the pot. "I was in really good shape when we put all the money in the pot."

Gutshot—See "Inside straight draw."

Hand—Your cards, or the process of dealing the cards until the winning of a given pot. "Boy, that hand took a while."

Heads-up—A situation in which poker is played one-on-one, mano a mano. Some people like heads-up better than a full table. "I played Freddy Bonyadi heads-up and lost $75,000!"

High-society chip—A poker chip worth $100. In the movie *Rounders*, Matt Damon's character says, "Give me three racks of high-society chips." A rack holds 100 chips, so Matt ordered $30,000 worth of chips!

High stakes—The level of play where the betting rounds are typically $75–$150 or higher. See "Low stakes."

Hit a card—Catch a good card, or a card that wins the pot for you. See "Catching a card."

Hold'em—Texas Hold'em, the world's most popular poker game. Each player is dealt two cards facedown, and the players share the five community cards dealt faceup in the middle of the table. The best five-card hand wins.

Hole—See "Position."

Hole cards—A player's two private facedown cards, which only he can see.

Home-style poker—See "Family poker game."

Horse (HORSE)—A game in which you play equal numbers of hands (or equal lengths of time) in five different games: Hold'em, Omaha Eight or Better

(High-Low Split), Razz (Seven-Card Low), Seven-Card Stud, and Seven-Card Stud High-Low Split (the letter E derives from eight or better). Horse is very popular in the poker community right now.

Hot—Winning more than one's share of pots. "Wayne Tyler sure was running hot today."

Implied odds—The odds that a player factors into his calculation of pot odds to account for being called if you complete your hand.

Inside straight draw—A straight draw in which a card of only one rank will complete your hand; otherwise known as a "Belly buster" or "Gutshot." For example, you complete an inside straight when an eight is dealt to complete a 7-8-9-10-J straight, an outcome twice as unlikely as filling an open-ended straight. Compare "Open-ended straight draw."

In the dark—Making a move without having looked at your facedown hole cards. "Stuart Skorman bet $80 in the dark."

In the money—Among the paying positions in a poker tournament. See "Money-cutoff line."

Isolation—A technique in which a player reraises a weaker player's bet, trying to play him heads-up (one on one) by making it expensive for any other players to call.

Jackal—A crazy, seemingly illogical player who makes

a lot of bets and raises. One of the "animal personalities" that I use to teach you poker strategy.

Jam—Bet and raise as many times as you can in a particular hand or round of betting, in order to increase the size of the pot.

Joker—In poker parlance, the perfect draw card. "Bonetti hit the joker again."

Judgment fold—Folding a hand on the basis of your read of all the factors involved.

Kicker—In a hand whose value lies in a pair, the highest other card. "Doyle Brunson won the pot with treys with a king kicker."

Ladies—A pair of queens.

Late position—The player on the button and the two players to the right of the button; these are positions of advantage in the course of play.

Lay down—Fold. "He just made a great lay down!"

Limit poker—A variation of poker games in which the amounts of the bets are preset, in contrast to no-limit poker, where you can bet any amount at any time. See also "Pot-limit."

Limping in—Calling the big blind bet before the flop.

Lion—A very tough, consistently winning poker player. One of the "animal personalities" that I use to teach you poker strategy.

Live hand—A hand that hasn't been folded or declared folded.

Locked up—Winning, with no chance of losing.

Loose—A style of play in which you play a lot of hands. "Here comes Ted Forrest. Man, can he play loose sometimes!"

Low stakes—The level of play where the betting rounds are typically $2 or lower. See "High stakes."

Made hand—A completed hand that is a straight or better.

Majority play—A term I use to refer to certain Hold'em hands, including all small pairs (six down to two), A-x suited, and K-Q. These hands are less promising but playable in certain circumstances.

Maniac—A loose, aggressive player who likes to raise a lot of pots. See also "Jackal."

Marginal-play hand—A somewhat weak hand that probably should not be played, according to the odds.

Mess with (another player)—Raise an opponent when holding a weak hand, in order to give the impression that you are a wild, loose player.

Missing—Failing to complete your hand. "I can't believe that Huck Seed missed his draw again!"

Money-cutoff line—The point in a poker tournament at which a player is guaranteed money if he survives that point. For example, twentieth place if the tournament pays 20 players deep.

Money game—A nontournament game, or side game. Participants in a money game play for cash.

Mouse—A supertight player who always has a strong hand when he bets and is thus often predictable. One of the "animal personalities" that I use to teach you poker strategy.

Move all-in—See "All-in."

Multiway pot—A hand in which more than two players are involved.

NLH—No-limit Hold'em.

No-limit—A variation of poker games in which players may bet as much as they want whenever it is their turn to play, as opposed to limit poker, where there is an established betting structure. See also "Pot-limit."

No-limit Hold'em—Often referred to as the Cadillac of poker. Players may bet any amount at any time. See "No-limit."

Nosebleed—Metaphor for high-stakes games in which players can lose large amounts of money very quickly. "Chip Reese is playing in the nosebleed games."

Nuts—In Hold'em, the best possible hand, given the faceup cards and their match to your hole cards.

Odds—The percentage chance that a player will win a given pot.

Off suit—Having hole cards of different suits, like As-Qh.

Online poker—Poker played on the Internet.

On the end—On the last card or last round of betting.

On tilt—See "Tilt."

Open a hand—Be the first bettor after the blinds have been posted.

Open-ended straight draw—A draw in which a player can hit one of two different cards to complete a straight. For example, a player with 8-9-10-J has an open-ended straight draw because he will hit the straight if either a seven or a queen comes. Compare "Inside straight draw."

Out, outer—The number of cards available to make a hand. If any ace is needed to win, then you have four outs (Ac-As-Ad-Ah). If a seven is needed to win, but you already have 7d in your hand, then it is a three-outer (7s-7c-7h).

Overcard—A card on the board of higher rank than the rank of the pair you have.

Overpair—A pocket pair of higher rank than the common cards on the board. If the board is J-6-2, then a hand of Q-Q is an overpair. "I swear Layne Flack always has an overpair!"

Over the top—Where you are when you reraise an opponent. A term usually used in no-limit Hold-'em. "I came over the top of him for all my chips."

Paint—A face card, whether jack, queen, king, or ace.

Pair—Two cards of the same rank, such as 4c-4h.

Phil's hand—A pair of black nines as hole cards, known as my hand because I won the WSOP with them.

Pip—Lose a pot in a very close hand.

PLH—Pot-limit Hold'em. See "Pot-limit."

Pocket pair—A pair as a player's facedown cards, such as 5c-5h.

Pocket rockets—A pair of aces as a player's facedown cards.

Position—Where a player is seated, relative to the button. The names of the positions at a nine-player table are, from left to right: button, small blind, big blind, 1 hole, 2 hole, 3 hole, 4 hole, 5 hole, 6 hole.

Positional advantage—Sitting behind an opponent in a hand, thus in position to act after the opponent acts.

Posting—Putting up an ante; in Hold'em, the fixed amounts put up by the two blinds.

Pot—The money gathered in the middle of the table during a hand.

Pot-limit—A variation of poker games in which the maximum bet a player may make is the size of the pot at the time the bet is made.

Pot-limit Hold'em—See "Pot-limit." "There is a great pot-limit Hold'em game at Artichoke Joe's Casino on Friday nights."

Pot odds—A calculation of odds: the size of the pot divided by the cost of calling a bet. Making a doubtful call or raise with a huge pot is more justified than making such a call with a small pot.

Presto—A pair of fives as a player's facedown cards. The name was coined by an online newsgroup, rec.gambling.poker.com (RGP).

Protecting your hand—Raising or betting to eliminate opponents and increase chances of winning with a strong hand. "Johnny Chan knows how to protect his hands."

Puck—The actual, physical button used to designate the "dealer." See "Button."

Putting in a bet—Making a bet.

Rabbit hunting—Looking to see what cards would have come up, after all players have folded their hands. This is considered bad etiquette in poker, because it slows the game down. However, some TV shows look at the "next" card!

Rack (of chips)—A container that holds 100 chips, all

of one designated value. Sometimes players use "rack" to describe the amount won or lost. "Last night Daniel Negreanu won two racks."

Rag—A weak or unplayable card. Small community cards can be referred to with this term. "The flop was all rags."

Raise—Match an opponent's bet and add a bet to it.

Ram and jam—Raise and reraise as much as you can in a given hand. "Phil Ivey sure did ram and jam that hand."

Reading (an opponent)—Making your best guess at what your opponent's hand is by studying his body language as well as his play and the dynamics of the hand.

Representing—Pretending that (and playing as if) you have a strong hand. "Huck Seed bet all his chips while representing a flush."

Reraise—Match and raise someone who has raised. "I reraised Steve and he folded his hand!"

Respecting—Knowing that your opponent has an imposing track record, believing that he has a good hand, and acting accordingly. "I give Doyle Brunson a lot of respect when I play a hand against him."

Restealing—Reraising a player who you believe is attempting a steal (he's weak), to try to bluff him out of a hand.

RGP—An online poker newsgroup: rec.gambling-
.poker.com.

River—See "Fifth street."

Rivered it—Made your hand on the river (last card).
"John Juanda rivered the ace-high flush."

Royal flush—An ace-high straight (A-K-Q-J-10), all of
the same suit, the best hand to be had in Hold'em.

Rushing—Winning pot after pot. "Alan Cunningham
was on a nice rush the other day."

Satellites—Ten-handed minitournaments in which
players put up one-tenth of the buy-in to a
subsequent poker tournament and the last player
standing (actually, the last person sitting!) wins a
seat in that event.

Second nuts—The second-best-possible hand.

Set—Three of a kind. This is a very popular term in
pokerese. "At the 1999 world championships, Huck
Seed flopped a set and won a $700,000 pot."

Setting a trap—See "Trapping."

Sheriff—A player who habitually calls opponents
down to make sure they aren't bluffing.

Shorthanded—Having four or fewer remaining
players at the table.

Showing down—Flipping the hands faceup after all
the betting is complete.

Side game—A nontournament poker game. "David 'Chip' Reese is one of the greatest side-game players in the world."

Slider—Someone who frequently moves all his chips into a pot in no-limit Hold'em, usually a high-risk move.

Slot tournament—A tournament in which the object is to run up your balance in a slot machine. The term implies that no skill is required, since slot machines involve only luck.

Slow-playing—Underbetting a strong hand, in order to lure other players into calling and raising. See "Smooth-calling."

Slow-rolling—Flipping the winning hand faceup, late, after allowing someone else to believe he has won the pot. Slow-rolling is considered bad etiquette in poker and is usually not forgotten by the loser!

Small blind—The blind that is just left of the button. The small blind costs that player half the amount the big blind posts. "Dewey Weum reraised him from the small blind and won a huge pot."

Smooth-calling—Just calling someone else's bet when you have a strong hand, in order to lure your other opponents into the pot. See "Slow-playing."

Solid—Succeeding though playing very few hands; a strategy having connotations of emotional control and soundness of play. "Don't play any hands against David Gray; he's as solid as a rock."

Stakes—The amount of money being played for at a given time and table. "Lyle Berman plays high-stakes poker."

Stand—Stop letting someone bluff you out, because you're sick of it. "Russ Hamilton called him, feeling it was time to make a stand!"

Stealing the blinds—In Hold'em, on the first round of betting, making a raise in hopes of forcing the blind hands to fold, thus winning the pot immediately. "Men 'The Master' Nguyen kept stealing my blinds today."

Stone-cold bluff—A bluff made while holding a very weak hand and no draw at all. "I can't believe that Meng La was on a stone-cold bluff again."

Straight—Five cards in unbroken number order, such as A-2-3-4-5 or 7-8-9-10-J, not all of the same suit.

Straight draw—See "Inside straight draw" and "Open-ended straight draw."

Straight flush—Five cards in a row all of the same suit, such as 3s-4s-5s-6s-7s or 8h-9h-10h-Jh-Qh, a hand exceeded in value only by a royal flush or by a straight flush of higher card rank.

Street—One complete round of betting, including the card that was dealt preceding the betting. "Monsieur Matloubi plays fifth street really well."

Sucking wind—A stretch of time when someone is just plain unlucky. You seem to miss your drawing hands, and your opponents seem to hit theirs.

Suit—The symbol appearing next to the rank number or letter on each card. The lowest suit is clubs, followed by diamonds, hearts, and spades. The letters c-d-h-s, the correct order of suits in breaking a tie, are in alphabetical order, the lowest letter designating the lowest-ranked suit.

Suited—Having your two hole cards of the same suit, such as 10h-Kh.

Suited connectors—Two hole cards of the same suit and of successive number rank, such as 9c-10c.

Supertight—Entering play only when holding one of a few select hands, such as A-A or K-K. For example, you may decide to play only my "top ten hands." See "Tight."

Swing—The roller-coaster ride that your chips may take on any given day when you play poker. "I watched Bobby Baldwin take a $450,000 swing yesterday. He went from $100,000 loser to $350,000 winner."

Table image—The way the other players at the table view you and your play. "Dave 'Devilfish' Ulliott had a really fast and loose table image today."

Taking one card off—Calling a bet or bets in order to see one more card—it's implied that if the next card doesn't help you, you'll fold.

Taking two cards off—Calling a bet or bets with the intent of seeing two more cards.

Texas Hold'em—See "Hold'em."

Three-betting—Making it three bets to go; raising when it's already two bets to go. "Hans 'Tuna' Lund kept three-betting me all day long."

Three of a kind—Three cards of the same rank, such as 2h-2s-2c or 7h-7d-7c. Commonly referred to as "trips" or "set."

Tight—Poker strategy in which you are very selective in choosing hands to play and thus play very few hands. "John Inashima plays so tight that I knew he had my hand beat." See "Supertight."

Tilt—When someone is playing far too many hands, and playing many poorly, because he's emotionally unbalanced. "In the 1993 World Championships, I tilted off my last $100,000." "After a crushing disappointment, Harry was on tilt all night."

Toothpick principle—The idea that you can enter a poker game with a tiny amount of money and end up with a small fortune. "Surrindar Sunar started with a toothpick and ended up with a lumberyard!"

Top kicker—The best possible high card to go with your pair. For example, with a board of 5-6-A, having A-K in the hole would yield top pair (aces) and top kicker (the king).

Top pair—A pair represented by the highest community card on the board. Thus, if the board is J-6-2, a pair of jacks would be top pair. "I had top pair, but I lost to Stu Ungar, who had top pair with an ace kicker."

"Top ten hands"—My best Hold'em hole cards: A-A, K-K, Q-Q, A-K, J-J, 10-10, 9-9, 8-8, 7-7, and A-Q.

Trapping (setting a trap)—Trying to trick an opponent into thinking you have a weak hand when in fact you have a powerful hand. To cleverly disguise your hand, causing your opponent to call you rather than folding. "John Bonetti really trapped him on that hand."

Treys—Pocket threes or one pair of threes.

Tricky—Playing hands in unorthodox ways to confuse your opponents. "Toto Leonidas is so tricky that many players never know what he has!"

Trips—A common term for three of a kind.

Turn (the turn)—The fourth card turned up on the board, and the action after the card is turned up. Also called "fourth street." "Simon 'Aces' Trumper always seems to catch the perfect card on the turn against me!" "I bet on the turn every pot, but no one ever called me."

Turned it—Made a hand on the fourth card. "Tony Dee turned a full house and won a big pot."

Undercard—A card of lower rank than others.

Underpair—A pair lower in rank than the cards on the board. For example, you have 5-5 in your hand and the board is J-8-7.

Under the gun—The position of the player directly to the left of the big blind, thus first to act, in ignorance of all other hands.

Value betting—Making a bet in the belief that you'll win money with what you hold slightly more often than you'll lose money with it. A bet that you may well lose, but you believe the chances favor your making the bet.

Wheel—In Hold'em, a five-high straight.

World Series of Poker (WSOP)—Roughly 30 poker tournaments, the last of which is a $10,000 buy-in event called the World Championship of Poker. The WSOP is the biggest and most prestigious series of poker tournaments in the world.

WSOP—The World Series of Poker, played at Binion's Horseshoe for over thirty years and now held at the Rio Hotel and Casino, with the final table still being played at the Horseshoe.

Zone—The almost mythical place or mind-set in which you're reading players perfectly and making all the right moves. "Phil was in the zone when he won at the World Series of Poker."

Acknowledgments

Thanks to my amazing wife, Kathy, for supporting me as I travel around the world playing poker for a living. Thanks to my children, Phillip III and Nick, for putting up with Daddy's line, "Don't talk to me while I write my book." Thanks to Andy Glazer, who was the single biggest help to me in writing and editing this book. Andy gave me two weeks of full-time help with this book and made it much better—and much more readable. In fact, Andy's fingerprints are all over this book. Thanks to uber-editor Bill Carver (a true master), whose changes and improvements are everywhere. Thanks to my sister Kerry Hellmuth who gave me a ton of time nailing down the glossary. Thanks to Jason Karl for the illustrations and charts that he created. Thanks to Jon Karl for smoothing out Chapter 8. A special thanks to my agent Sheree Bykofsky and my editor on *Play Poker Like the Pros*, Matthew Benjamin, for having faith in me and believing I could finish this book.

Index